M000232013

Miss Daisy's
BLUE RIBBON
DESSERTS

DAISY KING

HILLSBORO PRESS
Franklin, Tennessee

For Caroline Gettelfinger,
my precious friend who always wishes
she could eat dessert first.

———————————

Printed in the United States of America

04   03   02   01   00   1   2   3   4   5

Library of Congress Catalog Card Number: 00-108199

ISBN: 1-57736-212-8

Cover photo by John Russell

Cover design by Gary Bozeman

Specialty Tours quote written by Donna Rice for the Origins of Southern Cuisine tour.

HILLSBORO PRESS
PROVIDENCE HOUSE PUBLISHERS
238 Seaboard Lane • Franklin, Tennessee 37067
800-321-5692
www.providencehouse.com

Contents

Preface & Acknowledgments

My sweet life began when my grandmother taught me how to bake her favorite cake—I prepared it when I was six years old with a hand mixer and a wire whisk. Except for the vanilla extract, all of the ingredients were gathered from our family farm. As I grew older, she patiently showed me how to prepare many recipes for which she had won blue ribbons at county fairs. One of her blue ribbon pound cakes was always a must in our home. That pound cake was the beginning of my lifelong love of southern food.

In food development class in college, I added several additional flavor extracts to her pound cake recipe, and Miss Daisy's Five Flavor Pound Cake was born. This easily prepared and long-lasting cake has since graced countless tables throughout the South and its legacy continues with the recipe on page 121. It's also available at many local supermarkets.

My culinary career has taken me down numerous paths since my pound cake was created. The years I spent teaching food classes were always highlighted by introducing my students to new desserts. Miss Daisy's Restaurant, which I operated for seventeen years, served so many delicious sweets that patrons would often review the dessert menu as soon as they were seated. The viewers of the television shows on which I appear always write in for my scrumptious dessert recipes. Therefore, I thought it was appropriate that my first volume in a new series of cookbooks be *Miss Daisy's Blue Ribbon Desserts*.

This collection of my favorite desserts—simple recipes with ingredients that are accessible in your local supermarket—are blue ribbon winners in the seven dessert categories. I have collected these recipes over the years, waiting for the opportunity to share them with my faithful readers.

As you stroll through these pages of temptingly delicious sweets, know that they were chosen for a reason. They all have a southern twist, of course, because this is the area in which I have always lived. You'll find the recipes loaded with fruits and nuts grown in the South, as well as other essential ingredients like fresh eggs, butter, and cream—the same things my grandmother and I cooked with on the farm. I've written the directions so that any beginning cook will be able to achieve mouth-watering results with minimal time and effort. I've also included some helpful hints and blue ribbon tips with valuable information on preparation and serving suggestions.

This book would not have been possible without the sharing, support, and expertise of so many people. First, I must extend loving appreciation to my family and a universe of friends who have shared innumerable recipes with me over the past twenty-six years. My sons, Kevin and Patrick, have been especially cheerful when I tested recipes, and are always thankful for everything I cook. My mother-in-law, Mrs. Herman King, is a constant help; her advice and years of experience have made many of these recipes better.

The Gettelfinger families in Knoxville, Tennessee, have a fine heritage of family foods. Chris and Jill, Herman and Nancy, and Andrew and Chickie have been wonderful leaders in launching the exciting new line of Miss Daisy's Classic Southern Foods™, and I am eternally grateful for their vision, friendship, and support.

I am thankful for the skill and cooperation of Culinary Resources Group. They have helped me test and enhance many of the recipes contained in this book—guaranteeing that the exquisite flavor of each of the Miss Daisy's items is maintained as they produce them for your local supermarket.

A special thank-you to Dennis Perkins, who has been a helpful assistant in many endeavors, and is always there with a smile.

The staff at Providence House Publishers has produced this book with great expertise. I'm so thankful for my friends there, especially Andrew B. Miller, president and publisher, and each of his excellent staff members.

Gail Pittman has done a superb job of designing stunning serving pieces with a southern affinity. Examples of her artistry are featured on the cover of this book.

Many thanks to Kim Owens, who graciously allowed me to use her gorgeous kitchen as the backdrop for the book cover.

I know there are those whose names I haven't mentioned. To all of you, my heart is full of appreciation for all your kindness and support.

I hope you'll enjoy these recipes as much as I have, and that you'll share them with family and friends. Happy eating!

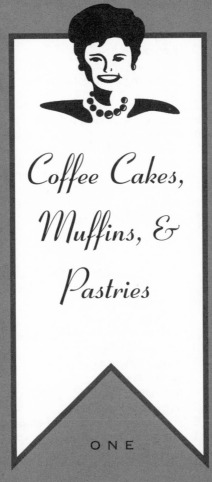

Coffee Cakes, Muffins, & Pastries

ONE

COFFEE CAKES 2 • MUFFINS 5
PASTRIES 7

Apricot Almond Coffee Cake

1	cup butter, softened
2	cups sugar
2	eggs
1	cup sour cream
1½	teaspoons almond extract
2	cups all-purpose flour
1	teaspoon baking powder
¼	teaspoon salt
1	cup sliced almonds
1	10-ounce jar apricot preserves

Assemble ingredients and utensils. In the large bowl of a mixer, combine butter and sugar until fluffy. Beat in eggs one at a time. Fold in sour cream and almond extract. Sift together flour, baking powder, and salt; fold into butter mixture. Place a third of the mixture in a greased and floured bundt or tube pan. Sprinkle half of the almonds and half of the preserves over the batter. Spoon on the remaining batter and add the remaining preserves. Top with the remaining almonds. Bake in a preheated 350° oven for 50 to 60 minutes or until done. Cool. Yield: 12 to 14 servings.

Peachy Coffee Cake

⅓	cup whole milk
1	package dry yeast
2	tablespoons warm water
¾	cup plus 2 tablespoons sugar
1	egg, lightly beaten
½	teaspoon salt
¾	cup butter, softened
2	cups all-purpose flour
8	fresh medium-to-ripe peaches, peeled and sliced
1	teaspoon ground cinnamon

Assemble ingredients and utensils. In a heavy saucepan, bring milk to boiling point; cool to lukewarm. Dissolve yeast in warm water; let stand 5 minutes. Add cooled milk, 2 tablespoons sugar, egg, and salt; stir to blend. In a separate bowl, cut ½ cup butter into flour; add milk and yeast mixture; beat until smooth. Spread into buttered 15x10x1-inch jelly roll pan. Let rise in warm place until double in bulk, about 1 hour. Arrange peach slices in rows on top of dough. Mix ¾ cup sugar and cinnamon; sprinkle over peaches; dot with ¼ cup butter. Bake in a preheated 375° oven for 20 minutes. Yield: 16 servings.

Sour Cream Coffee Cake

1   cup butter, softened
1¼ cups plus 4 tablespoons sugar
2   eggs
1   cup sour cream
1   teaspoon vanilla
2   cups all-purpose flour
1   teaspoon baking powder
1   teaspoon salt
1   teaspoon ground cinnamon
1   cup chopped nuts, pecans or walnuts

Assemble ingredients and utensils. In the large bowl of a mixer, combine butter and 1¼ cups sugar; add eggs, sour cream, and vanilla. Sift flour, baking powder, and salt together; stir into first mixture. Pour half the batter into a greased bundt or tube pan. Combine remaining ingredients; sprinkle half over batter. Pour on remaining batter and top with remaining sugar mixture. Bake in a preheated 350° oven for 1 hour. Yield: 10 to 12 servings.

HELPFUL HINT

When giving Sour Cream Coffee Cake as a gift, accompany it with a jar of coffee beans.

Coffee Cake Muffins

1½ cups all-purpose flour, sifted
½   cup sugar
2   teaspoons baking powder
½   teaspoon salt
¼   cup shortening
1   egg, beaten
½   cup whole milk

Spicy Nuts
½   cup brown sugar
½   cup pecans, chopped
2   tablespoons all-purpose flour
2   teaspoons ground cinnamon
2   tablespoons butter, melted

Assemble ingredients and utensils. In a small bowl, combine all ingredients for the spicy nuts; set bowl aside. In another mixing bowl, combine dry ingredients for muffins. Cut in shortening with pastry blender or 2 knives until mixture resembles coarse crumbs. In a small bowl, combine egg and milk. Add all at once to flour mixture; stir just until moistened. Alternate layers of batter and nut mixture into greased or paper-lined muffin tins, filling two-thirds full. Bake in a preheated 375° oven for 15 to 20 minutes. Yield: 12 muffins.

Cream Cheese Coffee Cake

1   18¼-ounce package of lemon cake mix
4   eggs
1   cup plus 1 tablespoon all-purpose flour
1   envelope dry yeast
⅔   cup plus 1 tablespoon warm water
2   8-ounce packages cream cheese, softened
¼   cup sugar
1   tablespoon whole milk
6   tablespoons butter, softened
1   cup confectioners' sugar
1   tablespoon light corn syrup

Assemble ingredients and utensils. In the large bowl of a mixer, combine 1½ cups of cake mix, 2 eggs, 1 cup flour, dry yeast, and ⅔ cup warm water; beat well for 2 minutes. Spread in greased 9x13-inch baking pan. In a separate bowl, combine cream cheese, 2 eggs, ¼ cup sugar, 1 tablespoon flour, and milk; beat until well blended. Spoon over batter in baking pan. In a small bowl, cut butter into remaining cake mix with pastry blender or 2 knives; sprinkle over cream cheese mixture. Bake in a preheated 350° oven for 40 to 45 minutes. In a small bowl, combine confectioners' sugar with corn syrup and 1 tablespoon water; mix well. Drizzle over hot coffee cake. Yield: 12 to 15 servings.

Coffee cakes are sweetened breads that are enjoyed at teatime, snack time, or even breakfast. They are normally individual-sized cakes, or they can be served in rings. Some are filled with fruit, while others are topped with pecans, glazes, or a dusting of sugar.

A NOTE FROM

Miss Daisy

Cranberry Nut Muffins

2 cups all-purpose flour
¼ cup sugar
1 teaspoon baking powder
½ teaspoon salt
1 egg, beaten
1 cup whole milk
¼ cup butter or shortening, melted and cooled
2 teaspoons orange zest, grated
½ cup fresh cranberries, washed and halved
⅓ cup pecans, chopped

Assemble ingredients and utensils. In the large bowl of a mixer, combine first 4 ingredients. Add remaining ingredients and stir only enough to moisten dry ingredients; do not overmix. Fill greased or paper-lined muffin tins two-thirds full. Bake in a preheated 400° oven for 20 to 25 minutes or until lightly browned. Yield: 10 to 12 muffins.

~

Strawberry Muffins

½ cup butter
1 cup sugar
2 eggs
2 cups all-purpose flour
1 teaspoon ground cinnamon
1 teaspoon ground nutmeg
1 teaspoon baking powder
½ cup whole milk, heated to lukewarm temperature
2 teaspoons apple cider vinegar
1 cup strawberry preserves

Assemble ingredients and utensils. In the large bowl of a mixer, combine butter and sugar until fluffy; add eggs one at a time and beat well after each addition. In a separate bowl, combine flour, cinnamon, nutmeg, and baking powder. In another bowl, combine milk and vinegar; add alternately with dry ingredients to butter and sugar mixture. Allow to sit for a few minutes; mix in preserves. Fill greased or paper-lined muffin tins two-thirds full. Bake in a preheated 375° oven for 20 minutes. Yield: 18 to 24 muffins.

Lemon Muffins

1 cup sugar
5 tablespoons butter
2 eggs
  zest of 1 lemon, grated
½ cup whole milk
½ teaspoon salt
1½ cups all-purpose flour
1 teaspoon baking powder
½ cup pecans, chopped

Glaze

  juice of 1 lemon
½ cup sugar

Assemble ingredients and utensils. In the large bowl of a mixer, combine sugar and butter until light and fluffy. In a separate bowl, beat eggs; add lemon zest and milk. Add egg mixture to creamed butter and sugar mixture; mix well. In a separate bowl, sift dry ingredients together and stir into creamed butter and sugar mixture, stirring only until there are no traces of dry ingredients remaining. Batter will be somewhat thick. Stir in pecans and spoon batter into 12 greased or paper-lined muffin tins. Bake in a preheated 350° oven for 25 to 30 minutes until golden. To prepare glaze while muffins bake, combine lemon juice and sugar; allow mixture to sit so that some of the sugar will dissolve. When muffins are baked, use a toothpick and make some holes in top of each muffin and pour the glaze over each hot muffin. Yield: 12 muffins.

Summer Blueberry Muffins

1½ cups self-rising flour
¾ cup sugar
¾ cup whole milk
⅓ cup oil
¾ cup fresh blueberries

Assemble ingredients and utensils. In the large bowl of a mixer, combine all ingredients except blueberries, and mix well. Stir in blueberries. Drop from a tablespoon to fill greased or paper-lined muffin tins two-thirds full. Bake in a preheated 400° oven for 25 minutes. Yield: 12 muffins.

Bite-Size Cinnamon Rolls

1	cup whole milk
1½	packages dry yeast
1	cup butter, melted and cooled
¾	cup sugar
1	egg, beaten
3½–4	cups all-purpose flour
2	teaspoons ground cinnamon

Assemble ingredients and utensils. In a small saucepan, scald milk (bring to boiling point) and then cool to lukewarm. Add yeast; when it bubbles, mix with ½ cup butter, ¼ cup sugar, and egg. Turn into a larger bowl; add flour until it makes a soft dough. Knead on floured board for 10 minutes. Place dough in a greased bowl and slightly butter top of dough; cover with a damp cloth. Let rise in a warm place for 1 hour; punch down. Roll out to ¼-inch thickness. In a separate bowl, combine ½ cup sugar and cinnamon. For bite-size rolls, cut dough with a small ½- to ¾-inch cutter. Dip each piece in remaining ½ cup of melted butter; roll in cinnamon sugar mixture. Put each piece on a flat pan; cover and let rise for 1 hour. Bake in a preheated 375° oven for 25 to 30 minutes. When done, remove from pan; cool. Top with glaze, if desired. Yield: 30 to 36 rolls.

Glaze

2½	cups confectioners' sugar
5	tablespoons whole milk

Assemble ingredients and utensils. In the small bowl of a mixer, combine sugar and milk; beat until smooth. Drizzle over cinnamon rolls.

Orange Sticky Buns

¼ cup plus 2 tablespoons sugar
2 tablespoons orange juice
2 tablespoons corn syrup
1 teaspoon orange zest, dried
1 8-ounce can crescent rolls
4 teaspoons butter, softened
⅛ teaspoon ground cinnamon

Assemble ingredients and utensils. In the large bowl of a mixer, combine ¼ cup sugar, orange juice, syrup, and ½ teaspoon orange zest. Spoon 1 tablespoon of mixture into each of 8 greased or paper-lined muffin tins, or 1½ teaspoons into each of 16 small tins. Separate crescent dough into 2 rectangles. Spread each rectangle with 2 teaspoons butter. In a small bowl, mix 2 tablespoons sugar, ½ teaspoon orange zest, and cinnamon for the filling; sprinkle over dough. Starting at the shorter side, roll together. Cut into either 8 or 16 slices, depending on which size pans are used. Place cut side down in tins. Bake in a preheated 375° oven for 20 to 25 minutes. Invert immediately. Yield: 8 or 16 servings.

Doughnuts have experienced a new surge in popularity in recent years, owing primarily to the growth of franchised doughnut shops. Many upscale restaurants have joined the trend by serving yeast-raised doughnuts, similar to the recipe on the following page.

A NOTE FROM

Miss Daisy

Glazed Doughnuts

1 cup very warm liquid (½ cup water and ½ cup whole milk)
2 packages dry yeast
¼ cup shortening (shortening and butter are a great combination here)
⅓ cup plus 1 tablespoon sugar
1 teaspoon salt
2 teaspoons vanilla
¼ teaspoon lemon extract
4–4½ cups all-purpose flour, sifted
1 large egg
    cooking oil for deep frying

A TIP FROM

Miss Daisy

After you mix the dough, if you refrigerate the dough for about an hour, it is easier to handle. The more egg yolks in the doughnut dough, the less grease they will absorb when fried.

Assemble ingredients and utensils. In a small bowl, soften yeast in liquid. In the large bowl of a mixer, when yeast is softened, combine yeast and shortening (and butter); break apart with a spoon. Add sugar, salt, and flavorings. Stir in enough flour (about 2½ cups) so that you can beat batter until very smooth. Add egg; beat again. Gradually add more flour until stiff enough to turn out and knead. Knead until smooth and elastic; dough will be soft. Return to lightly greased bowl; cover and let rise until double. Turn out on floured surface and roll to ½-inch thick; cut with doughnut cutter. Place on lightly greased cookie sheet; let rise again (about 1 hour). In a heavy saucepan or pot filled about half full with oil or shortening, drop doughnuts in to fry, turning with a fork to brown on both sides. After they are brown, remove from the hot oil and dip into glaze; continue procedure until all doughnuts are completed. Yield: 18 to 20 doughnuts.

Glaze
¾ of 16-ounce box confectioners' sugar
    whole milk
1 tablespoon vanilla flavoring
3 drops vanilla extract

Assemble ingredients and utensils. In a medium bowl, add enough milk to three fourths of the box of confectioners' sugar to mix well and smooth out the lumps. Gradually add more milk until thin enough to dip doughnuts. You want this glaze to be about the thickness of pancake syrup. Stir in 1 tablespoon vanilla and 3 drops vanilla extract.

Popovers

1   cup all-purpose flour
½   teaspoon salt
1   cup whole milk
2   eggs
    ground cinnamon and confectioners' sugar for
        garnish

Assemble ingredients and utensils. In a small bowl, beat the ingredients until smooth. Pour into well-greased or paper-lined deep muffin tins until they are three-fourths full, or oven-proof glass cups until half full. Bake in a preheated 425° oven for 35 to 40 minutes until golden brown. Serve immediately. Sprinkle with cinnamon and confectioners' sugar. Yield: 6 to 8 popovers.

~

Chocolate-Filled Eclairs

A NOTE FROM

Miss Daisy

Heavy cream
is also called
whipping
cream, and
half-and-half
can be called
light cream.

½   cup water, boiling
¼   cup butter
½   cup all-purpose flour, sifted
¼   teaspoon salt
2   eggs
1   cup heavy cream
¼   cup sugar
1   tablespoon cocoa
    confectioners' sugar
    chocolate glaze (see p. 131)

Assemble ingredients and utensils. In a heavy saucepan with boiling water, add butter; reduce to medium heat. Add flour and salt all at once, stirring vigorously until dough leaves side of pan in a smooth mass. Remove from heat. Beat in eggs one at a time. Beat until smooth and stiff. Form dough into six oblong shapes with wet spoon or knife; place 3 inches apart on greased cookie sheet. Bake in a preheated 450° oven for 20 minutes; reduce oven temp to 350° and bake for additional 10 minutes until golden brown. Cool. Whip heavy cream until stiff, beating in cocoa and sugar. Split eclairs; fill with whipped cream; dust with confectioners' sugar or glaze with chocolate glaze. Yield: 6 eclairs.

Swedish Puff Pastry

First layer
1   cup all-purpose flour
½   cup butter
2   tablespoons water

Second layer
½   cup butter
1   cup water
1   teaspoon almond extract
1   cup all-purpose flour
3   eggs

Glaze
¼–⅓   cup whole milk
1   cup confectioners' sugar
     almonds, toasted

Assemble ingredients and utensils.

First layer: In a small bowl, cut butter into flour with pastry blender or 2 knives until the mixture resembles coarse cornmeal; add water; roll into 2 logs. Pat logs into 2 12x3-inch rectangles on ungreased cookie sheet. The rectangles should be about 3 inches apart.

Second layer: In a saucepan, heat butter and water together and bring to a boil. Add almond extract and remove from heat. Add flour all at once; blend until smooth. Add eggs one at a time, beating well after each addition. Spread this on top of the first layer. Bake in a preheated 400° oven for 5 minutes. Reduce heat to 350° and continue baking for 45 minutes.

Glaze: In a saucepan, heat the milk, add confectioners' sugar; beat until smooth. Pour over warm pastry and sprinkle with toasted almonds. Yield: 12 servings.

Apple Fritters

1½ cups all-purpose flour
2 tablespoons sugar
1 teaspoon baking powder
½ teaspoon salt
2 tablespoons cooking oil
1 egg, beaten
1 tablespoon whole milk
½ teaspoon vanilla
¼ teaspoon ground nutmeg
1 tart apple, peeled
  cooking oil for deep-frying
  confectioners' sugar for garnish

Assemble ingredients and utensils. In the large bowl of a mixer, combine flour, sugar, baking powder, and salt; make a well in center of mixture and add oil, egg, and milk; mix well. Add vanilla and nutmeg. Grate apple on the large side of grater and stir into batter. Refrigerate batter overnight. Fry in deep oil by heaping spoonfuls; drain fritters on paper towels. Just before serving, pour lemon sauce over fritters and sprinkle with confectioners' sugar. Yield: 20 to 24 fritters.

Lemon Sauce

1 egg, beaten
4 tablespoons butter
  juice of 2 lemons
1 cup sugar
½ cup water

Assemble ingredients and utensils. In a heavy saucepan, mix all ingredients and cook over low heat until thick and syrupy. This will keep in the refrigerator for about a week. Yield: 1½ cups sauce.

Fried Pies

2	8-ounce packages dried peaches or apples
1½	cups sugar
	water

Assemble ingredients and utensils. In a saucepan, cover the dried fruit with water and cook until the fruit is tender. Mash with potato masher and add sugar; set aside while making the crust dough.

Crust Dough

2	cups all-purpose flour
1	teaspoon salt
⅓	cup shortening
½–¾	cup buttermilk
	shortening for deep frying

Assemble ingredients and utensils. In a medium mixing bowl, combine flour and salt; cut in shortening with a pastry blender or 2 knives until the mixture resembles coarse corn-meal. Gradually add ½ to ¾ cup buttermilk as needed to make the dough stiffer than regular dough. Take a ball of dough the size of a biscuit and roll it out on a floured surface to less than ⅛-inch thickness. Cut a round circle using a saucer for the pattern. Place a heaping teaspoon of the fruit on one side of the crust near the center; fold the other side over it and seal the edges with a fork. Prick the top in 3 places with the tines of a fork. Place the pie in hot shortening about 3 inches deep, prefer-ably in an iron skillet. Fry until golden brown on one side; turn and fry on the other side; drain on paper towels. Yield: 8 pies.

A TIP FROM

Miss Daisy

Chill pastry or pie dough in freezer for 5 minutes or in refrigerator for 10 minutes to reduce amount of flour needed on board when rolling out. Excess flour results in a tough crust.

Apricot Pastries

1   8-ounce package cream cheese
1   cup butter
2   cups all-purpose flour
1   16-ounce jar apricot jam
    granulated sugar for garnish

Assemble ingredients and utensils. In the large bowl of a mixer, combine cream cheese and butter until soft. Add flour with hands until blended and firm. Roll out half of dough on a sheet of waxed paper to fit a cookie sheet. Lift carefully and invert on cookie sheet, pulling waxed paper off. Spread with apricot jam. Roll out the second half of dough and lay on top of the jam. Pinch sides together to seal well. Prick top layer with fork and pat with water. Sprinkle with granulated sugar. Bake in a preheated 350° oven for 35 to 40 minutes. Cool. Cut into squares. Yield: 12 to 14 pastries.

~

Pecan Tassies

3   ounces cream cheese
½   cup plus 1 tablespoon butter
1   cup all-purpose flour
1   egg
¾   cup brown sugar
1   teaspoon vanilla
⅛   teaspoon salt
⅔   cup pecans, finely chopped

Assemble ingredients and utensils. For the cream cheese pastry: let the cream cheese and ½ cup butter soften to room temperature; blend together in the large bowl of a mixer. Stir in flour; chill about 1 hour. Shape into 24 1-inch balls. Place in ungreased 1¾-inch mini-muffin tins; press dough evenly against bottom and sides of each. For filling: in the medium bowl of a mixer, beat together egg, brown sugar, 1 tablespoon butter, vanilla, and salt until smooth. Divide half of the pecans among pastry-lined tins; add egg mixture; top with remaining pecans. Bake in a preheated 325° oven for 25 to 30 minutes, or until filling is set. Cool before removing from pans. Yield: 24 pastries.

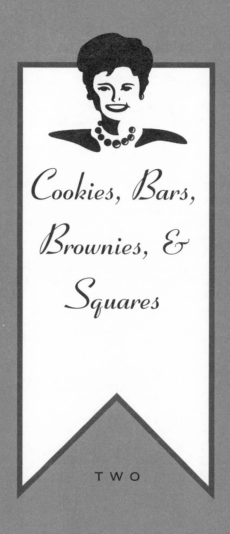

Cookies, Bars, Brownies, & Squares

TWO

Grandma's Sugar Cookies

HELPFUL HINT

To make sour milk, use 1 tablespoon vinegar plus whole milk to equal 1 cup.

2   cups sugar
1   cup shortening
2   eggs
1   teaspoon vanilla
1   teaspoon lemon extract (optional)
1   teaspoon baking soda
1   cup sour whole milk
4–5 cups all-purpose flour
2   teaspoons baking powder
1   teaspoon ground nutmeg
    sugar for garnish

Assemble ingredients and utensils. In the large bowl of a mixer, blend sugar and shortening. Add eggs one at a time, beating well after each addition; add vanilla and lemon extract. In another bowl, dissolve baking soda in milk; sift 4 cups flour with baking powder and nutmeg. Add sour milk and flour alternately to creamed mixture. Add enough additional flour to make dough easy to handle. Chill dough for 2 hours. Flour hands and pastry board. Roll out dough about ¼ - to ½-inch thick; cut with a 2- to 3-inch cookie cutter. Place cookies on greased cookie sheets, sprinkle with sugar. Bake in a preheated 400° to 425° oven for 8 minutes or until lightly browned. Watch carefully. Yield: 72 cookies.

Southern Tea Cakes

2¼ cups all-purpose flour, sifted
¼   teaspoon salt
2   teaspoons baking powder
½   cup butter
1   cup sugar
2   eggs, beaten
½   teaspoon vanilla
1   tablespoon whole milk

Assemble ingredients and utensils. Sift flour, salt, and baking powder together. Mix butter, sugar, and eggs until creamy consistency. Add remaining ingredients and combine with flour mixture. Blend well. Roll dough out on floured board to ½-inch thickness. Use cookie cutter to cut out shapes. Place on an ungreased cookie sheet. Bake in a preheated 350° oven for 12 to 15 minutes or until lightly browned. Yield: 24 tea cakes.

Shortbread Wedges

1   cup butter or margarine
¼   cup sugar
½   teaspoon vanilla
2½   cups all-purpose flour

Assemble ingredients and utensils. In the large bowl of a mixer, combine butter, sugar, and vanilla until light and fluffy. Stir in flour. Divide dough in half. Pat each half into a 7-inch diameter circle. Place on an ungreased cookie sheet. Prick dough with fork to make pie-shaped wedges. Bake in a preheated 325° oven for 20 to 25 minutes or until lightly golden. Cool 1 minute; place on wire rack to cool. Break into wedges. Yield: 16 servings.

~

Scottish Shortbread Cookies

2¼   cups all-purpose flour
¼   teaspoon salt
1   cup butter, softened
½   cup sugar
1   teaspoon vanilla
     cinnamon sugar for garnish
     confectioners' sugar for garnish

Assemble ingredients and utensils. In a small bowl, combine flour and salt. In the large bowl of a mixer, combine softened butter, sugar, and vanilla; mix until smooth. Stir in dry ingredients. Knead on a very lightly floured board. Wrap dough in aluminum foil or plastic film; chill for 1 hour. Divide dough into 2 parts; roll out ¼-inch thick and into a 9x6-inch rectangle on a lightly floured board. Cut into 1½-inch squares, triangles, or any fancy shape with a cookie cutter. Imprint center with a fancy design or points of a dinner fork. Place on ungreased baking sheet; sprinkle with cinnamon sugar before baking, or with confectioners' sugar on warm cookies after baking. Bake in a preheated 325° oven for 15 to 20 minutes or until delicately browned. Yield: 24 to 36 cookies.

Oatmeal Cookies

HELPFUL HINT

Keep soft cookies soft by placing a slice of bread in the container that they're being kept in.

1½ cups all-purpose flour
1 teaspoon baking powder
1 teaspoon baking soda
½ teaspoon salt
1 cup shortening
1½ cups light brown sugar
½ cup sugar
2 eggs
1 teaspoon vanilla
3 cups quick-cooking rolled oats
1 cup nuts
confectioners' sugar

Assemble ingredients and utensils. Sift flour, baking powder, baking soda, and salt together. In the large bowl of a mixer, combine shortening, sugars, eggs, and vanilla. Add to flour mixture. Stir in oats and nuts. Form balls and shake in a bag of confectioners' sugar to coat. Place on a greased cookie sheet and press with a fork. Bake in a preheated 350° oven for 12 to 15 minutes or until light brown. Yield: 18 to 24 cookies.

Peanut Butter Jumbos

1 cup butter or margarine
1 cup peanut butter
1 cup sugar
1 cup brown sugar, firmly packed
2 eggs
2 cups all-purpose flour
1 teaspoon baking soda
1½ cups candy-coated chocolate-covered peanut candies

Assemble ingredients and utensils. In the large bowl of a mixer, beat together butter, peanut butter, and sugars until light and fluffy; blend in eggs. In another bowl, combine flour and baking soda; gradually add to peanut butter mixture. Stir in candy-coated chocolate-covered peanut candies. Drop dough by level ¼ cup measures onto greased cookie sheet, about 3 inches apart. Press 3 to 4 additional candies into each cookie, if desired. Bake in a preheated 350° oven for 14 to 16 minutes, or until edges are golden brown. Cool cookies on sheet for 3 minutes; remove to wire rack until completely cool. Yield: 24 cookies.

Macaroons

1   cup almond paste
2/3   cup sugar
1/4   cup confectioners' sugar
2   tablespoons all-purpose flour
1/8   teaspoon salt
1/2   teaspoon almond extract
1/4   cup egg whites, unbeaten

Assemble ingredients and utensils. Break almond paste into very small pieces, and in a large bowl, mix in sugar, confectioners' sugar, flour, salt, and almond extract, adding just enough egg whites to make a very stiff mixture. Drop heaping teaspoonfuls 2 inches apart on a baking sheet lined with ungreased wax paper or lightly greased aluminum foil. Bake in a preheated 325° oven for 20 minutes, or until set; remove from the oven and let stand for 2 minutes. Set paper or foil on damp cloth to loosen the macaroons for easy removal. Yield: 24 macaroons.

Almond Paste
3 1/4   cups whole blanched almonds
2   cups confectioners' sugar
1/3   cup egg whites, unbeaten
1   tablespoon almond extract
1   teaspoon vanilla

Assemble ingredients and utensils. In a food processor or blender, beat almonds until very fine. In a mixing bowl, combine almonds and confectioners' sugar; add remaining ingredients and blend thoroughly (mixture will be very stiff). Yield: 3 cups almond paste.

Cathedral Window Cookies

1   12-ounce package chocolate chips
1/2   cup butter
1   10-ounce package colored miniature marshmallows
1   cup walnuts, chopped
1   7-ounce package sweetened flaked coconut

Assemble ingredients and utensils. In the top of a double boiler, melt chocolate chips and butter; cool. Add marshmallows and nuts. Divide mixture in half and form 2 large rolls. Roll in coconut and wrap in wax paper. Chill for 24 hours. Slice 1/2-inch thick to serve. Yield: 36 cookies.

A NOTE FROM

Miss Daisy

Macaroons are a crunchy confection made of almond paste, sugar, and egg whites. They were introduced to this country in New Orleans by the early French settlers.

Coconut Butterballs

A TIP FROM

Miss Daisy

Baking
sheets with
little or no
sides will let
your cookies
bake evenly
and quickly.

½ cup butter, softened
2 tablespoons confectioners' sugar
1 teaspoon vanilla
1 teaspoon orange zest, grated
1 cup all-purpose flour
¾ cup sweetened flaked coconut
   confectioners' sugar for coating

Assemble ingredients and utensils. In the large bowl of a mixer, combine butter, sugar, vanilla, and orange zest; mix until fluffy. Stir in flour and coconut. Chill for about 10 minutes. Form dough into balls (use 1 rounded teaspoon for each ball); place balls 1 inch apart on ungreased baking sheet. Bake in a preheated 350° oven for 12 to 15 minutes, or until done. Transfer balls to wire rack to cool. Roll in confectioners' sugar while slightly warm. Yield: 42 balls.

~

Walnut Cookies

½ cup margarine or butter, softened
½ cup sugar
1 egg, separated
1 teaspoon lemon zest, grated
1 cup all-purpose flour
¼ teaspoon ground cinnamon
   pinch of ground cloves
1¾ cups walnuts, finely chopped
½ cup apricot preserves

Assemble ingredients and utensils. In the large bowl of a mixer, blend margarine and sugar, beating until light and fluffy. Add egg yolk and lemon zest; beat well. Combine dry ingredients and 1 cup walnuts; stir into creamed mixture. Cover dough and chill at least 30 minutes. Lightly beat egg white. Shape dough into 1-inch balls. Dip each ball in egg white, roll in remaining walnuts, and place on greased cookie sheet. With your thumb, make an indentation in the center of each cookie and fill with preserves. Bake in a preheated 350° oven for 15 minutes. Cool on wire rack. Yield: 36 cookies.

Crescents

1   cup butter
¾   cup sugar
2   teaspoons vanilla
2½   cups all-purpose flour
1   cup pecans or almonds, ground
      confectioners' sugar for coating

Assemble ingredients and utensils. In the large bowl of a mixer, beat butter until light; gradually add sugar and mix until fluffy. Beat in vanilla; gradually blend in flour and nuts. Chill dough thoroughly so it will handle easily. Form teaspoonfuls of dough into crescent shapes. Place ¾-inch apart on ungreased baking sheet. Bake in a preheated 350° oven for 12 to 15 minutes, or until lightly browned. Cool slightly and remove from baking sheet; while warm, roll in confectioners' sugar. Cool on rack. Yield: 90 to 96 crescents.

~

Holiday Cookies

1   cup butter
2   cups light brown sugar
2   eggs
1   teaspoon vanilla
½   cup buttermilk
3½   cups all-purpose flour
1   teaspoon baking soda
1   teaspoon salt
1½   cups pecans, chopped
1   cup sweetened flaked coconut
2   cups candied cherries, halved
1   cup dates, chopped

Assemble ingredients and utensils. In the large bowl of a mixer, combine butter, sugar, eggs, and vanilla thoroughly; stir in buttermilk. In a separate bowl, sift dry ingredients together; then add to wet mixture. Stir in nuts, coconut, cherries, and dates. Chill at least 1 hour. Drop by teaspoonfulls 2 inches apart onto lightly greased baking sheet. Bake in a preheated 400° oven for 8 to 10 minutes. Yield: 24 cookies.

Thumbprint Cookies

¾ cup butter
3 ounces cream cheese
2 cups all-purpose flour
2 tablespoons sugar
½ teaspoon salt
¼ teaspoon baking powder
½ cup jam or jelly of your choice

Assemble ingredients and utensils. In the large bowl of a mixer, combine butter and cream cheese; beat until light and fluffy. In a separate bowl, sift together flour, sugar, salt, and baking powder; stir into butter and cream cheese mixture. Roll out on lightly floured surface into a square about ½-inch thick; cut into 1½-inch squares. Place on ungreased baking sheet, and with your thumb make an indentation in the center of each cookie. Fill with ½ teaspoon of your favorite jam or jelly. Bake in a preheated 350° oven for 20 to 25 minutes. Yield: 30 cookies.

HELPFUL HINT

Children will enjoy making these cookies because they can use their imaginations.

Cocoa Kiss Cookies

1 cup butter
⅔ cup sugar
1 teaspoon vanilla
1⅔ cups all-purpose flour
½ cup cocoa
1 cup pecans, finely chopped
1 9-ounce package milk chocolate kisses (about 54 per package)

Assemble ingredients and utensils. In the large bowl of a mixer, combine butter, sugar, and vanilla; beat until fluffy. Beat in flour and cocoa gradually. Add nuts and beat at low speed until evenly distributed. Chill in the bowl for 30 minutes. Unwrap chocolate kisses. Shape a teaspoon of dough around each chocolate kiss; roll in your palms and pinch away excess dough to make a small ball. Place a few inches apart on ungreased cookie sheet. Bake in a preheated 375° oven for 10 to 12 minutes or until set; do not overbake. Cool. Yield: 48 to 50 cookies.

No-Bake Cookies

1 cup light corn syrup
1 cup sugar
1 12-ounce jar peanut butter
1 cup sweetened flaked coconut
5 cups flaked corn cereal
1 cup pecans, chopped (optional)

Assemble ingredients and utensils. In a heavy saucepan, combine corn syrup and sugar and bring to a rolling boil; remove syrup mixture from heat and stir in peanut butter until smooth. In a large bowl, place coconut, cereal, and pecans; pour syrup mixture over them and mix. Drop by spoonfuls on waxed paper; chill. Yield: 42 to 48 cookies.

Orange Coconut Crisps

2 eggs
2/3 cup salad oil
1 cup sugar
1/4 cup frozen orange juice concentrate, thawed
   (do not dilute)
2½ cups all-purpose flour, sifted
2 teaspoons baking powder
½ teaspoon salt
1 cup sweetened flaked coconut

A TIP FROM

Miss Daisy

A bunch of homemade cookies in a large mixing bowl makes a nice gift.

Assemble ingredients and utensils. In the large bowl of a mixer, beat eggs lightly; stir in oil and sugar; beat until mixture thickens; stir in orange juice. Sift flour into a separate bowl, then measure. Sift measured flour with baking powder and salt. Add flour mixture and coconut to egg mixture; mix well. Drop teaspoons of dough about 2 inches apart onto an ungreased baking sheet. Press each cookie flat with the bottom of a drinking glass that has been oiled lightly with salad oil and dipped in sugar. Dip the glass in sugar before flattening each cookie. Bake in a preheated 400° oven for 8 to 10 minutes, or until the cookies are a delicate brown (a slight dent shows when you touch top lightly with fingertip). Remove pan from oven and take cookies from baking sheet with a wide spatula. Spread cookies on wire rack to cool. Yield: 36 cookies.

Lemon Tea Cookies

2   teaspoons lemon juice
½   cup whole milk
1¾ cups all-purpose flour
1   teaspoon baking powder
¼   teaspoon baking soda
¼   teaspoon salt
½   cup butter or margarine
¾   cup sugar
1   egg
1   teaspoon lemon zest, finely grated

Assemble ingredients and utensils. Combine lemon juice and milk. Sift next 4 ingredients together. Blend butter and sugar, beating until light and fluffy. Add egg and lemon zest. Add flour mixture and milk mixture alternately to the batter, beating well after each addition. Drop by rounded teaspoonfuls 2 inches apart onto an ungreased cookie sheet. Bake in a preheated 350° oven for 12 to 14 minutes. Cool cookies on wire rack. Spread with lemon icing. Yield: 48 cookies.

Lemon Icing

1¾ cups confectioners' sugar, sifted
1   tablespoon butter, melted
2   tablespoons lemon juice
2   drops yellow food coloring

Assemble ingredients and utensils. Combine all ingredients until well blended. Spread on cooled cookies.

Lemon Thins

1   cup butter
½   cup sugar
1   egg, beaten
2   cups all-purpose flour
½   teaspoon baking powder
⅛   teaspoon salt
1   tablespoon lemon juice
1   teaspoon lemon zest, grated

HELPFUL HINT

Lemon Thins are great to accompany Chocolate Rum Ice Cream (see p. 66).

Assemble ingredients and utensils. In the large bowl of a mixer, combine butter and sugar until light and fluffy; add egg and mix well. Combine flour, baking powder, and salt and add to sugar mixture; mix well. Add lemon juice and lemon zest; mix again. Form into rolls 1½ to 2 inches in diameter; wrap tightly in clear wrap or foil; chill. Slice very thin. Place 1½ inches apart on ungreased baking sheet. Bake in a preheated 375° oven for 7 to 10 minutes. Remove cookies and cool. Yield: 72 cookies.

~

Old-Fashioned Molasses Cookies

½   cup butter, softened
⅓   cup brown sugar
1   egg
½   cup molasses
¼   cup whole milk
2   cups all-purpose flour
½   teaspoon salt
½   teaspoon ground ginger or ground cloves
½   teaspoon ground cinnamon
1   teaspoon baking soda

Assemble ingredients and utensils. In the large bowl of a mixer, blend butter and sugar until fluffy. Add egg, molasses, and milk. Sift remaining ingredients together and add to butter mixture. Blend well. Mixture should be stiff. If mixture is too thin, add more flour. Spoon onto well-greased cookie sheets, leaving space for spreading during baking. Bake in a preheated 375° oven for 10 minutes. Yield: 36 to 48 cookies.

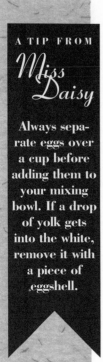
Apricot Almond Bars

⅔ cup dried apricots
½ cup butter, softened
¼ cup sugar
1⅓ cups all-purpose flour
1 cup light brown sugar, firmly packed
2 eggs, well beaten
½ teaspoon baking powder
¼ teaspoon salt
½ teaspoon vanilla
½ cup almonds, chopped

Assemble ingredients and utensils. Rinse apricots; cover with water and simmer 10 minutes. Drain, cool, and chop. In a large bowl, combine butter, sugar, and 1 cup flour; mix until crumbly. Pack into a greased 9-inch square pan. Bake in a preheated 350° oven for 20 minutes. In the large bowl of a mixer, gradually beat brown sugar into eggs. Sift together remaining flour, baking powder, and salt; add to egg mixture and mix well. Add vanilla, ¼ cup almonds, and apricots. Spread on baked layer; sprinkle with remaining nuts. Bake in a preheated 350° oven for 20 to 25 minutes. Cool in pan; cut into 1½-inch squares. Sprinkle with confectioners' sugar. Yield: 28 to 30 bars.

Chocolate Chip Bars

1 cup butter
1 cup light brown sugar, firmly packed
1½ teaspoons vanilla
⅛ teaspoon salt
2 cups all-purpose flour
1 6-ounce package semi-sweet chocolate chips
1 cup walnuts, chopped

Assemble ingredients and utensils. In the large bowl of a mixer, combine butter and sugar; mix until light; beat in vanilla. In a separate bowl, combine salt and flour; gradually stir into butter mixture; mixing well. Fold in chocolate chips and nuts. Press into ungreased jelly roll pan or flat baking pan approximately 16x10x1-inch. Bake in a preheated 350° oven for 20 minutes. Cool. Cut into 2½x1½-inch bars. Yield: 36 bars.

Peanut Butter Logs

1   cup butter, melted
½   cup crunchy peanut butter
1½   cups quick-cooking rolled oats
1   teaspoon vanilla
1   16-ounce box confectioners' sugar
½   cup raisins
1   cup sweetened flaked coconut

Assemble ingredients and utensils. In a large bowl, mix all ingredients well and shape into 24 to 30 logs. Glaze with the following.

Glaze
1   6-ounce package semi-sweet chocolate chips
2   ounces paraffin

Assemble ingredients and utensils. In the top of a double boiler, melt chocolate and paraffin. Dip logs in glaze and place on waxed paper to dry. Yield: 24 to 30 logs, depending on size.

Vienna Chocolate Bars

1   cup butter, softened
1½   cups sugar
2   egg yolks
2½   cups all-purpose flour
1   10-ounce jar raspberry jelly or apricot preserves
1   cup semi-sweet chocolate chips
4   egg whites
¼   teaspoon salt
2   cups pecans, finely chopped

Assemble ingredients and utensils. In the large bowl of a mixer, combine butter with ½ cup sugar and egg yolks; mix until light and fluffy. Add flour and knead in bowl with fingers. Pat batter out on greased cookie sheet to ¾-inch thickness. Bake in a preheated 350° oven for 15 to 20 minutes until lightly browned; remove from oven. Spread with jelly or preserves and top with chocolate chips. In the small bowl of a mixer, beat egg whites with salt until stiff; fold in remaining cup of sugar and nuts. Carefully spread on top of jelly and chocolate. Bake in a preheated 350° oven for an additional 25 minutes. Cut into 3x1-inch squares. Yield: 24 bars.

Fudge Nut Bars

1	cup plus 2 tablespoons butter, softened
2	cups light brown sugar, packed
2	eggs
2	teaspoons vanilla
2½	cups all-purpose flour, sifted
1	teaspoon baking soda
1½	teaspoons salt
3	cups quick-cooking rolled oats
1	12-ounce package semi-sweet chocolate chips
1	cup sweetened condensed milk
1	cup nuts, chopped

Assemble ingredients and utensils. In the large bowl of a mixer, combine 1 cup butter and brown sugar. Add eggs, one at a time, beating well after each addition. Add 1 teaspoon vanilla. Combine flour, soda, and 1 teaspoon salt; stir into creamed mixture. Stir in oats. Spread about two-thirds of oat mixture in bottom of 9x12-inch pan. Set aside. Combine chocolate chips, milk, 2 tablespoons butter, and ½ teaspoon salt in saucepan. Cook over low heat, stirring until mixture is smooth. Remove from heat, add nuts and remaining vanilla. Spread over layer in pan. Dot with remaining oat mixture, spreading as evenly as possible. Bake in a preheated 350° oven for 25 to 30 minutes, or until lightly browned. Cool and cut into bars. Yield: 24 bars.

Double Chocolate Brownies

4	1-ounce squares unsweetened baking chocolate
1	cup butter
4	eggs
1	cup sugar
1	cup light brown sugar
1½	cups all-purpose flour
1	teaspoon baking powder
2	teaspoons vanilla
1	cup pecans or walnuts, or mixed, chopped
½	cup miniature marshmallows

Assemble ingredients and utensils. In the top of a double boiler, melt chocolate and butter. In a large bowl, beat eggs, add sugars, then flour sifted with baking powder. Stir in vanilla and nuts, then chocolate mixture. Turn into a greased and lightly floured 15x10x1-inch pan. Bake in a preheated 325° oven for 25 to 30 minutes. Prepare frosting. Remove from oven; immediately spread marshmallows over top, then frost. Yield: 72 brownies.

Frosting

½	cup butter
3	1-ounce squares unsweetened baking chocolate
1	cup sugar
5	ounces evaporated milk
1	16-ounce box confectioners' sugar
1	teaspoon vanilla

Assemble ingredients and utensils. Do not wash the double boiler chocolate pot. Add to it ½ cup butter, chocolate, sugar, and evaporated milk. Cook in double boiler until well blended. Beat in sugar and vanilla. Pour immediately over hot marshmallow-covered brownies. Cool for 4 hours. Cut and serve.

A TIP FROM

Miss Daisy

Never measure liquids like vanilla or almond extract directly over the mixing bowl—it could easily overflow the measuring spoon and spill into the recipe.

Frosted Mocha Brownies

2   1-ounce squares unsweetened chocolate
⅓   cup butter
2   eggs
1   cup sugar
1   teaspoon vanilla
¾   cup all-purpose flour
¾   teaspoon baking powder
¼   teaspoon salt
2   tablespoons instant coffee powder
¾   cup pecans, chopped

Assemble ingredients and utensils. In a heavy saucepan over low heat, melt chocolate and butter, stirring constantly; set aside to cool. In the large bowl of a mixer, beat eggs until light; gradually add sugar; beat until fluffy; add vanilla. Combine with chocolate mixture and mix well. In a separate bowl, combine flour, baking powder, salt, and coffee powder; stir into chocolate mixture and mix well. Fold in pecans. Pour into a greased 8-inch square pan. Bake in a preheated 350° oven for 25 to 30 minutes, or until light imprint remains when fingertips touch center. Cool. Add mocha frosting. Cut into 2-inch squares. Yield: 16 squares.

Mocha Frosting

1   1-ounce square unsweetened chocolate
1   tablespoon butter
2   tablespoons strong brewed coffee, very hot
1   cup confectioners' sugar, sifted

Assemble ingredients and utensils. In a heavy saucepan, melt chocolate with butter, stirring constantly; blend in coffee and about 1 cup confectioners' sugar. Mix enough to make a frosting that spreads smoothly and easily.

∼

Marbled Brownies

⅔ cup all-purpose flour, sifted
½ teaspoon baking powder
½ teaspoon salt
4 1-ounce squares sweet baking chocolate
⅓ cup butter
3 ounces cream cheese, softened
1 cup sugar
3 eggs
1 tablespoon vanilla
⅔ cup pecans, chopped
confectioners' sugar for garnish

HELPFUL HINT

These keep well in the refrigerator.

Assemble ingredients and utensils. In a small bowl, sift together flour, baking powder, and salt. In a heavy saucepan, combine chocolate and 3 tablespoons butter; melt over very low heat, stirring constantly until chocolate is melted; cool. In the large bowl of a mixer, beat remaining butter and cream cheese thoroughly; add ¼ cup sugar gradually, beating well after each addition. Add 1 egg, beat until fluffy; set aside. In another bowl, beat remaining 2 eggs; add the remaining ¾ cup sugar and vanilla; and continue beating until very thick and fluffy. Stir in cooled chocolate and the dry ingredients; fold in pecans. Alternate spoonfuls of chocolate mixture and cheese mixture into a greased and floured 9x9x2-inch baking pan. Using a knife, fold the chocolate mixture over the cheese mixture to marbleize batter. Bake in a preheated 350° oven for 45 minutes, or until inserted toothpick comes out clean. Cool in pan for 5 minutes before removing. Sprinkle with confectioners' sugar. Cut into squares. Yield: 16 squares.

A TIP FROM

Miss Daisy

Cookies or baked treats in seasonal containers make wonderful gifts. For instance, use a heart-shaped container on Valentine's Day, or a basket filled with cookies and recipes for Mother's Day. Try filling a copper mold, a ceramic bowl, a soufflé dish, or even an old-fashioned jar with cookies, brownies, breads, cakes, or candies.

Tennessee Brownies

A TIP FROM

Miss Daisy

These brownies are also good without the icing, in which case you should add the nuts to the batter.

1 cup butter or margarine
2 cups sugar
3 eggs
1 cup all-purpose flour
1 teaspoon baking powder
¼ cup cocoa
1 teaspoon vanilla
1½ cups nuts (optional)

Assemble ingredients and utensils. In a saucepan, melt butter. Pour butter into large bowl of mixer, add sugar and mix well. Add eggs, flour, baking powder, cocoa, vanilla, and nuts (if not used in icing). Pour into 13x9x2-inch pan. Bake in a preheated 350° oven for 30 minutes, or 25 minutes if using a glass baking dish. Cool and frost with icing. Yield: 12 to 16 servings.

Icing

½ cup butter or margarine
3 tablespoons cocoa
1½ tablespoons light corn syrup
18 large marshmallows
1 box confectioners' sugar
1 teaspoon vanilla
1½ cups nuts

Assemble ingredients and utensils. In a saucepan, combine butter, cocoa, corn syrup, and marshmallows over low heat, stirring until melted. Add confectioners' sugar, vanilla, and nuts. Pour over warm brownies.

Chess Pie Squares

1 ½   cups plus 1 tablespoon all-purpose flour
1 ¼   cups light brown sugar, firmly packed
1   cup butter (½ cup melted)
½   cup sugar
2   tablespoons whole milk
2   eggs
½   cup pecans, chopped
      confectioners' sugar for garnish

Assemble ingredients and utensils. In the large bowl of a
mixer, combine 1 ½ cups flour and ¼ cup light brown sugar;
cut in ½ cup butter using mixer on low speed until particles
are fine. Press mixture into bottom of ungreased 13x9x2-inch
pan. Bake in a preheated 375° oven for 10 minutes. In the
small bowl of a mixer, combine 1 tablespoon flour, 1 cup
brown sugar, ½ cup melted butter, and next four ingredients;
beat well. Pour over crust in pan. Bake in a preheated 375°
oven for 20 minutes, or until golden brown. Cool. Dust with
confectioners' sugar. Cut into 2-inch squares. Yield: 24
squares.

No-Bake Fruit Squares

1   cup raisins
½   cup dried apricots
½   cup dried figs
1   cup dates
½   cup candied orange peel
¼   cup candied cherries
1   cup walnuts, chopped
3   tablespoons orange juice
      confectioners' sugar

Assemble ingredients and utensils. Wash raisins, apricots, and
figs. In a food processor, grind first 7 ingredients together.
Add enough orange juice to hold the fruits and nuts together;
mix well. Press into greased 8x8x2-inch pan; chill several
hours or overnight. Cut into squares; coat squares with
confectioners' sugar. Yield: 24 pieces.

English Tea Squares

¾ cup butter
1 cup sugar
1 egg
1½ teaspoons vanilla
2 cups all-purpose flour, sifted
¼ teaspoon ground allspice
1 cup walnuts, chopped
½ cup strawberry jam
3 tablespoons confectioners' sugar

Assemble ingredients and utensils. In the large bowl of a mixer, beat butter until light and creamy in texture; add sugar and beat until fluffy. Beat in egg and vanilla, and blend well. Stir in flour, allspice, and walnuts. Spoon half of mixture into lightly greased 9-inch square pan; spread strawberry jam over top; spoon remaining half of mixture over jam. Bake in a preheated 350° oven for 40 to 45 minutes or until browned. Place on cooling rack and sift confectioners' sugar over the top. Cool. Cut into 1½-inch squares. Yield: 36 squares.

If you want to soften brown sugar that's as hard as a rock, put a slice of bread or half an apple in the package and close it tightly. In a couple of hours the brown sugar will be soft again. You can also soften it by putting it in the microwave.

A TIP FROM
Miss Daisy

Soufflés, Puddings, Custards, & Mousses

THREE

Chocolate Soufflé

3   1-ounce squares unsweetened chocolate
3   tablespoons brewed coffee, cold
3   tablespoons butter
3   tablespoons all-purpose flour
¾   cup whole milk, hot
⅓   cup sugar
⅛   teaspoon salt
4   egg yolks, lightly beaten
5   egg whites, stiffly beaten
    whipped cream for garnish

Assemble ingredients and utensils. In the top of a double boiler, melt chocolate with the coffee. In a saucepan over low heat, melt butter; blend in flour; gradually add the heated milk, sugar, and salt. Cook until mixture is smooth and thickened, stirring constantly, 45 minutes. Blend in the chocolate coffee mixture and the beaten egg yolks. Cool. Fold in stiffly-beaten egg whites. Pour mixture into 6 greased individual soufflé dishes which have been sprinkled with sugar; or use a 1-quart soufflé dish, greased and sugared, which will be about two-thirds full. Bake the individual soufflés in a preheated 300° oven for 10 to 12 minutes; bake the 1-quart soufflé in a preheated 375° oven for 30 to 40 minutes. Top with whipped cream. Serve immediately. Yield: 6 servings.

A soufflé base is a light, airy mixture that usually begins with a thick egg yolk–based sauce or puree that is lightened by stiffly beaten egg whites. Soufflés may be savory or sweet. Dessert soufflés may be baked, chilled, or frozen, and are most often flavored with fruit purees, chocolate, lemon, or liqueurs. They are customarily baked in a classic soufflé dish, which is round and has straight sides to facilitate the soufflé's rising.

Cold Lime Soufflé

1	envelope unflavored gelatin
¼	cup cold water
4	egg yolks
½	cup lime juice
½	cup sugar
½	teaspoon salt
1	tablespoon lime zest, grated
6	egg whites
½	cup sugar
1	cup heavy cream, whipped
	sweetened flaked coconut, lightly toasted, for garnish

Assemble ingredients and utensils. In a small bowl, sprinkle gelatin over water to soften. In the top of a double boiler, mix egg yolks, lime juice, sugar, and salt. Cook mixture over simmering water until slightly thickened; remove from heat. Stir in softened gelatin and lime zest; stir mixture until gelatin is completely dissolved. Cool. In a small bowl, beat egg whites until stiff; gradually beat in sugar until whites hold peaks. Fold whipped heavy cream and egg whites into lime mixture. Spoon into soufflé dish. Chill. Sprinkle with coconut flakes before serving. Yield: 4 to 6 servings.

Cold Strawberry Soufflé

4   envelopes unflavored gelatin
2   cups sugar
3   pints strawberries, pureed (about 3 cups)
8   eggs, separated
¼   cup fresh lemon juice
2   cups heavy cream, whipped
    sliced almonds, unblanched and toasted

Assemble ingredients and utensils. In a saucepan, mix the gelatin and 1 cup sugar, and stir in 1½ cups strawberries; mix in the beaten egg yolks. Cook over medium heat, stirring constantly, just until the mixture boils; remove from heat. Stir in remaining strawberries and lemon juice. Place the pan in the refrigerator or in a bowl of ice and water until the mixture mounds slightly when dropped from a spoon, about 15 to 30 minutes. In a small mixing bowl, beat egg whites until foamy; beat in remaining sugar 1 tablespoon at a time until the egg whites are stiff and glossy. Fold strawberry mixture into egg white mixture. Whip heavy cream in a chilled bowl until stiff; fold into the meringue mixture. Using a 2-quart soufflé dish or casserole, extend the height of the sides by securing a 4-inch band of double-thickness aluminum foil around the top rim. Carefully spoon mixture into the soufflé dish and swirl it on the top. Refrigerate. Just before serving, run edge of knife inside the foil and remove the band. Garnish the top and sides of soufflé with almonds. Yield: 16 servings.

Bread Pudding with Brandy Sauce

10 slices day-old bread, crusts removed
4 cups whole milk, scalded
1 cup heavy cream
4 eggs
1 cup sugar
1 teaspoon vanilla
1 teaspoon ground cinnamon
½ teaspoon ground nutmeg
¼ cup butter, melted
½ cup seedless raisins
   whipped cream for garnish

Assemble ingredients and utensils. In a large bowl, break bread into pieces and combine with milk and heavy cream. In another bowl, beat eggs; add sugar and the next 5 ingredients. Pour over bread mixture. Pour into a 3-quart baking dish; place dish into pan of warm water. Bake in a preheated 350° oven for 1½ hours. Serve brandy sauce over warm pudding and top with whipped cream. Yield: 8 servings.

Brandy Sauce
3 egg yolks
1 cup sugar
1 teaspoon vanilla
1½ cups whole milk
1 tablespoon cornstarch
¼ cup water
1½ ounces brandy

Assemble ingredients and utensils. In a saucepan, lightly beat yolks; add sugar, vanilla, and milk; heat. Blend cornstarch into water; stir into hot mixture. Continue cooking until thickened. Remove from heat and stir in brandy. Cool and serve over pudding.

A TIP FROM
Miss Daisy

For a ladies' luncheon, use a small nosegay of flowers at each place setting instead of a centerpiece.

Coffee Bread Pudding

1 cup strong brewed coffee
1 cup half-and-half
2 cups whole milk
6 thin slices raisin bread
¼ butter, softened
2 eggs
½ cup sugar
½ teaspoon salt
1 teaspoon vanilla
¼ teaspoon ground nutmeg
  whipped cream and grated chocolate for garnish

Assemble ingredients and utensils. In a heavy saucepan, combine coffee, half-and-half, and milk; bring to a scalding point (but do not boil). Spread bread slices lightly with butter; do not trim off the crust; cut in ½-inch cubes; add to coffee mixture. In a medium bowl, beat the eggs slightly; add sugar and salt; mix well; add the bread mixture and vanilla. Pour into greased 1½-quart casserole dish; sprinkle with nutmeg. Set the casserole dish in a pan of warm water. Bake in a preheated 325° oven for 1 hour and 15 minutes. Chill. Serve with whipped cream and garnish with grated chocolate on top. Yield: 8 servings.

Vanilla Pudding

½ cup sugar
2 tablespoons cornstarch
½ teaspoon salt
2 cups whole milk
2 egg yolks, lightly beaten
2 teaspoons butter
1 teaspoon vanilla

Assemble ingredients and utensils. In a heavy saucepan, mix sugar, cornstarch, and salt; gradually stir in milk. Cook over medium heat, stirring constantly, until mixture thickens and boils. Boil 1 minute; remove from heat. Gradually stir half of hot mixture into egg yolks; then blend egg yolk mixture into the mixture in the saucepan. Boil 1 minute more, stirring constantly; remove from heat. Blend in butter and vanilla. Serve warm or cool. Yield: 6 servings.

Old Recipe Banana Pudding

2   cups sugar
¼   cup all-purpose flour
½   teaspoon salt
4   cups whole milk
6   egg yolks, beaten
1   tablespoon vanilla
1   16-ounce package vanilla wafers
4   bananas, sliced
6   egg whites

Assemble ingredients and utensils. In the top of a double boiler, combine 1½ cups sugar, flour, and salt. Stir in milk. Cook over boiling water until thickened, stirring constantly. Remove from heat. Stir small amount of hot mixture, ¼ cup, into egg yolks. Return egg yolk mixture to hot mixture in double boiler. Cook over boiling water, stirring constantly for about 5 minutes. Remove from heat. Stir in vanilla. To assemble, layer wafers, bananas, and custard alternately in a 2-quart baking dish. Beat egg whites until stiff peaks form. Beat in ½ cup sugar. Spread over top of pudding. Bake in a preheated 350° oven for 8 to 10 minutes or until lightly browned. Yield: 10 to 12 servings.

Miss Daisy

The vanilla pudding recipe on the facing page comes from Marilyn Lehew. Marilyn is from Pennsylvania, where blueberries grow in abundance. Over the years, at her home and even at her restaurant, she has served blueberries—now Tennessee blueberries—with her vanilla pudding, which is a treat in itself.

Date Nut Pudding with Orange Sauce

1	tablespoon baking soda
½	cup buttermilk
2	cups sugar
2	cups butter
3½	cups all-purpose flour
4	eggs, beaten
1	cup pecans, chopped
1	cup dates, chopped
1	cup frozen flaked coconut

Assemble ingredients and utensils. In a small bowl, dissolve baking soda in buttermilk. In a large bowl, combine sugar and butter; add buttermilk mixture, flour, and beaten eggs; blend well. Add pecans, dates, and coconut. Spoon into a greased tube pan. Bake in a preheated 300° oven for 1½ hours. Pour orange sauce over the cake while cake is hot; cool before removing from pan. Yield: 10 to 12 servings.

Orange Sauce

1½	cups orange juice
½	cup sugar

Assemble ingredients and utensils. Heat orange juice and sugar over low heat until the sugar dissolves.

Easy Chocolate Pudding

2 1-ounce squares unsweetened baking chocolate
1 cup sugar
1 tablespoon all-purpose flour
⅛ teaspoon salt
1 cup whole milk
3 egg yolks, beaten
½ teaspoon vanilla
   whipped cream and raspberries to garnish

Assemble ingredients and utensils. In a heavy saucepan, melt chocolate on very low heat. In another saucepan, mix sugar, flour, and salt; add milk and heat until almost boiling. Add to melted chocolate. Take off heat; add small amount of milk mixture to egg yolks, stirring constantly. Return egg mixture to remaining milk, stirring constantly. Cook in the top of a double boiler until thick (but do not allow to boil). Remove from heat and add vanilla; chill. Top with real whipped cream and fresh raspberries. Yield: 4 to 6 servings.

Variation:
A meringue of egg whites may be spread on top of the pudding. If an egg white meringue is used, quickly place into a preheated 400° oven just until meringue is browned on top.

Grated Sweet Potato Pudding

4 eggs
2 cups sugar
1 teaspoon ground allspice
½ teaspoon ground cinnamon
¼ teaspoon ground cloves
¼ teaspoon salt
5 tablespoons butter or margarine, melted
2 cups whole milk
2 tablespoons vanilla
3 cups packed grated sweet potatoes (grate on
      smallest side of hand grater)

Assemble ingredients and utensils. In the large bowl of a mixer, beat eggs; add next 8 ingredients; blend well. Stir in grated sweet potatoes. Pour into a greased 2-quart casserole dish. Bake in a preheated 350° oven for 1–1½ hours. Yield: 8 to 10 servings.

A TIP FROM

Miss Daisy

Always keep the bottle of vanilla in the box in which it comes, because light or excessive heat will cause deterioration.

Crème Brûlée

2   cups half-and-half
1   cup heavy cream
¼   cup sugar
6   egg yolks, beaten
2   teaspoons vanilla
¾   cup light brown sugar
    fresh fruit for garnish

Assemble ingredients and utensils. In a heavy saucepan, heat half-and-half and heavy cream (but do not boil); add the sugar and stir until dissolved. Stir in the egg yolks and vanilla. Pour into a 7½-inch ovenproof bowl or soufflé dish. Place bowl in a pan of water. Bake in a preheated 300° oven for 50–60 minutes. Cool and chill thoroughly. About 2 hours before serving, sift brown sugar over the top to cover the custard completely. Preheat broiler to 350°. Set the custard bowl in a pan of ice and place about 6 inches below the broiler, moving it around constantly to melt the brown sugar but not to burn it. Cool slightly and return bowl to the refrigerator to chill. Serve as is or topped with any fresh fruit. Yield: 6 to 8 servings.

Coffee Chocolate Custard

1½   1-ounce squares semi-sweet chocolate, finely chopped
1   cup strong brewed coffee, hot
1   cup whole milk
4–6   tablespoons sugar
½   teaspoon salt
2   eggs

Assemble ingredients and utensils. In the large bowl of a mixer, pour hot coffee over chocolate; add milk, sugar, salt, and eggs. Blend and pour into 4 greased custard cups. Set a rack in a pan filled with an inch of hot—but not boiling—water. Place a folded towel on the rack and set custard cups on top of the towel. Bake in a preheated 325° oven for 20 minutes. To test for doneness, insert knife near the edge of cup. If blade comes out clean, the custard will be solid all the way through when cooled. Remove the custards from the pan and cool on a rack. Yield: 4 servings.

Coconut Orange Custard

4   egg yolks, well beaten
4   tablespoons sugar
1   tablespoon all-purpose flour
⅛   teaspoon salt
1   cup whole milk, scalded
1   teaspoon vanilla
1   cup heavy cream, whipped
    fresh orange sections
    fresh grated coconut

Assemble ingredients and utensils. In the top of a double boiler, combine egg yolks, sugar, flour, and salt; add milk; stir well. Cook over boiling water, stirring constantly until mixture thickens. Cool; add vanilla. Alternate the custard sauce and whipped cream with layers of orange sections and coconut in parfait glasses. Yield: 6 servings.

~

Holiday Custard

4   cups whole milk
6   eggs
1   cup sugar
2   teaspoons vanilla or brandy or liqueur of your choice
    ground nutmeg
    whipped cream or eggnog ice cream (optional)

Assemble ingredients and utensils. In a heavy saucepan, heat milk (but do not boil). In the small bowl of a mixer, combine eggs and sugar until blended. Add egg mixture to the hot milk, stirring constantly. Cook 5 to 7 minutes over medium heat, or until the custard begins to thicken. The custard will thicken further as it cools. Add vanilla, brandy, or other liqueur to cooled custard. Sprinkle a little nutmeg on top when you're ready to serve. Top with whipped cream or a scoop of eggnog ice cream. Yield: 5 cups.

A TIP FROM
Miss Daisy

To scald milk without scorching it, rinse the pan in hot water before using.

HELPFUL HINT

The key to a successful custard is low heat. High heat causes the eggs to curdle.

~

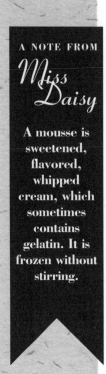
Pineapple Mousse

1 cup fresh pineapple, grated
juice of ½ lemon
3 egg yolks
½ cup sugar
⅛ teaspoon salt
1½ envelopes unflavored gelatin
½ cup whole milk
1 cup heavy cream, whipped
2 tablespoons cherry brandy
1 pint fresh strawberries, stems removed

Assemble ingredients and utensils. Grate pineapple with a
hand grater. Add lemon juice to grated pineapple. In a small
bowl, beat egg yolks, sugar, and salt until thick and lemon-
colored; add grated pineapple and mix well. In the top of a
double boiler, stir pineapple mixture until it thickens. In a
small bowl, sprinkle gelatin over cold milk, then add gelatin
mixture to hot pineapple mixture; stir to dissolve the
gelatin. Chill mixture until it thickens slightly; fold in
whipped heavy cream and cherry brandy. Chill until set.
Serve in individual soufflé dishes, champagne glasses, or
sherbet dishes; garnish with strawberries. Yield: 6 servings.

Elegant Chocolate Mousse

4 1-ounce squares unsweetened baking chocolate
8 eggs, separated
1 cup confectioners' sugar, sifted
1½ ounces bourbon
¾ cup heavy cream, whipped with 1 tablespoon
sugar and 1 teaspoon bourbon

Assemble ingredients and utensils. In a heavy saucepan, melt
chocolate. In a medium bowl, beat yolks, adding confectioners' sugar gradually, until yolks are pale yellow. Slowly
mix yolks into chocolate over low heat until very smooth.
Add bourbon. In a medium bowl, beat egg whites until almost
stiff. Gently fold whites into chocolate mixture until blended.
Refrigerate, covered, overnight. When ready to serve, top
with whipped heavy cream mixture. Yield: 8 servings.

Chocolate Coffee Mousse

½ cup sugar
½ cup water
2 eggs
   dash salt
1 6-ounce package semi-sweet chocolate chips
2 tablespoons cognac
3 tablespoons coffee liquer
½ pint heavy cream, whipped
   slivered almonds, toasted

Assemble ingredients and utensils. In a medium saucepan, heat sugar and water until dissolved. Set aside. Mix eggs, salt, and chocolate in blender. Slowly blend in sugar mixture until thick. Set aside until cool. Add cognac and coffee liquer. Fold in half of the whipped cream. Spoon into serving dishes or bowls. Chill for several hours before serving. Serve topped with remaining whipped cream and toasted almonds. Yield: 6 servings.

~

Ginger Pumpkin Mousse

4 eggs
7 tablespoons sugar
1 tablespoon unflavored gelatin
1½ cups canned pumpkin
¾ teaspoon ground cinnamon
½ teaspoon ground ginger
¼ teaspoon ground nutmeg
1 cup heavy cream, whipped
   minced crystallized ginger for garnish

Assemble ingredients and utensils. In a small mixing bowl, beat eggs with sugar until mixture is light-colored and thick; add gelatin and beat to blend well. Mix in pumpkin and spices. Chill mixture until it begins to set. In a small mixing bowl, whip heavy cream into soft peaks; fold into pumpkin mixture. Pour into 6 dessert dishes or a large serving bowl. Chill for 3 to 4 hours. Before serving, decorate with crystallized ginger. Yield: 6 servings.

Raspberry Mousse

1   10-ounce package frozen raspberries, thawed
¾   cup sugar
1   cup water
1   envelope unflavored gelatin
1   cup heavy cream, whipped
3   tablespoons cherry brandy
    whipped cream for garnish

Assemble ingredients and utensils. Puree raspberries using a blender or food processor and strain to remove the seeds. In a heavy saucepan, stir the sugar and ¾ cup water together. Boil without stirring until the syrup registers 240°F on a candy thermometer; cool slightly. Soften gelatin in ¼ cup water and add to hot syrup; stir until dissolved. Add the syrup to the raspberry puree; chill until syrupy, stirring occasionally. Whip heavy cream into soft peaks; fold in cherry brandy. When the raspberry mixture begins to thicken, fold in the whipped cream mixture. Quickly spoon mousse into cups, sherbets, or molds; chill. Top with additional whipped cream when serving. Yield: 6 servings.

Lemon Mousse

A TIP FROM

Miss Daisy

If your sauce is lumpy, whip briskly with a whisk, press through a strainer, or process briefly in a blender.

4   eggs, separated
1½ cups sugar
1   tablespoon unflavored gelatin, softened in ¼ cup
        cold water
1   teaspoon cornstarch
    juice of 3 lemons
    zest of 3 lemons, grated
¼   cup triple sec
1½ cups heavy cream
3   tablespoons confectioners' sugar

Assemble ingredients and utensils. In a medium bowl, beat egg yolks; add sugar and beat well. Set aside. Place gelatin mixture in the top of a double boiler and stir until dissolved. In another bowl, combine cornstarch and one-third of the lemon juice. Stir until smooth. Add to gelatin; stir in remaining juice and zest. Add beaten egg yolks. Cook until thickened, stirring constantly. Add half of the triple sec; cook 1 minute. Do not boil. Chill until set. In another bowl, whip heavy cream, remaining triple sec, and confectioners' sugar until stiff peaks form. Fold cream mixture and lightly beaten egg whites into lemon mixture. Spoon into soufflé dish; chill. Yield: 8 to 10 servings.

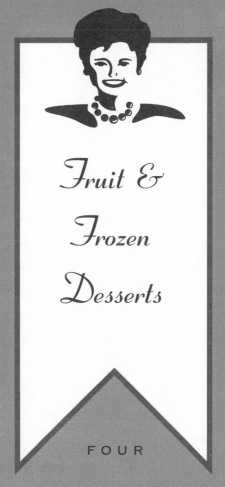

Fruit &

Frozen

Desserts

FOUR

Cinnamon Baked Apples

8   McIntosh or Rome Beauty apples, unpeeled,
     cored, and sliced into eighths
½–¾ cup light brown sugar (to taste)
1   teaspoon ground cinnamon
¼   cup butter
     whipped cream or ice cream (optional)

Assemble ingredients and utensils. Mix all ingredients together. Place in large glass baking dish, cover. Bake in a preheated 350° oven until apples are soft and tender, about 1 hour. Delicious served as a dessert with whipped cream on top, or as a sauce over ice cream. Yield: 8 servings.

Rum Raisin Apple Brown Betty

½   cup walnuts, coarsely chopped
2   cups coarse whole wheat bread crumbs
¼   cup oat bran
6   tablespoons butter
8   medium Granny Smith apples, peeled, cored, and
     thinly sliced (about 7 cups)
     juice of 1 lemon
1   tablespoon lemon zest, grated
1   cup light brown sugar
1   tablespoon cornstarch
1   teaspoon ground cinnamon
¼   teaspoon ground nutmeg
2   tablespoons dark rum
½   cup raisins, preferably dark
     whipped cream or ice cream (optional)

HELPFUL HINT

When using fruit zest or peel, always be careful not to include the bitter white part underneath. Use a fine grater, a vegetable peeler, or a special zester purchased at a cookware store.

Assemble ingredients and utensils. In a bowl, combine walnuts, bread crumbs, oat bran, and 5 tablespoons of melted butter; set aside. In a large bowl, combine apple slices, half the juice of 1 lemon, and all remaining ingredients, reserving remaining lemon juice and remaining 1 tablespoon butter. Spread a third of bread crumb mixture on bottom of buttered 2-quart casserole or soufflé dish. Add half of apple mixture. Repeat layers, ending with remaining bread crumb mixture. Sprinkle remainder of lemon juice over the top, and dot with remaining 1 tablespoon of butter. Cover with aluminum foil and bake in a preheated 350° oven for 20 minutes. Remove foil and bake 30 minutes longer. Top with whipped cream or ice cream. Yield: 6 servings.

The Best Baked Fruit

Sauce
⅓	cup butter
¾	cup brown sugar
1	tablespoon curry powder
⅛	teaspoon apple pie spice
1	teaspoon sherry or apple brandy (optional)

Fruit
2	30-ounce cans pear halves
1	30-ounce can sliced peaches
1	30-ounce can plums
1	16-ounce can pineapple chunks
1	16-ounce can blueberries
1	16-ounce can apricot halves
1	8-ounce can mandarin oranges
¼	cup almonds or walnuts, slivered

Assemble ingredients and utensils. For the sauce, place all the ingredients in a saucepan; heat until dissolved. Drain the fruits well and place in a 3-quart glass casserole dish. Pour sauce over fruit; cover. Bake in a preheated 300° oven for one hour. Yield: 10 to 12 servings.

A TIP FROM
Miss Daisy

Try these delicious ideas:
- Cantaloupe filled with fresh raspberries makes a delightful dessert.
- Honeydew melon quartered and filled with raspberry or lime ice is cool and refreshing.
- Melon balls served in chilled glasses and covered with champagne are heavenly.

Butter Rum Bananas

½ cup butter
1 cup sugar
¼ cup water
¼ cup dark rum
1 tablespoon lemon juice
   zest of 1 lemon, grated
1 teaspoon vanilla
8 small bananas
   ice cream (optional)

Assemble ingredients and utensils. In a heavy saucepan, melt butter; add sugar and water; cook until reduced to a heavy syrup. Add rum, lemon juice, zest, and vanilla. Peel and halve bananas lengthwise. Add to hot syrup and cover. Serve warm, not hot. Delicious served over ice cream. Yield: 8 servings.

Bananas Foster

3 (medium to ripe) bananas, sliced in chunks about 2½ inches long
3 tablespoons butter, melted
6 heaping tablespoons dark brown sugar
1 teaspoon ground cinnamon
6 tablespoons creme de banana (optional)
6 tablespoons dark rum

Assemble ingredients and utensils. In a heavy skillet, melt butter. Roll bananas in melted butter to coat on all sides; sprinkle with brown sugar and cinnamon; cook for 2 minutes, stirring constantly. Warm liqueurs in a separate saucepan. Remove bananas from heat. Pour warm liqueurs over bananas. Ignite, and spoon over vanilla ice cream. Yield: 6 servings.

Holiday Ambrosia

2   13½-ounce cans pineapple chunks
5   medium oranges
2   fully ripe bananas
2   cups white seedless grapes
1   3½-ounce can sweetened flaked coconut
    whole maraschino cherries
    sparkling soda (optional)

Assemble ingredients and utensils. Drain pineapple, reserving liquid. Pare oranges with a sharp knife and remove sections by cutting close to the membrane; squeeze and reserve any remaining juice. Peel bananas; slice and place with orange juice in a glass bowl. Add pineapple, oranges, bananas, and grapes separately; sprinkle with half of coconut. Pour reserved pineapple juice over all. Chill. When you're ready to serve, dot with remaining coconut and add maraschino cherries. Sparkling soda can be poured over all. Yield: 10 to 12 servings.

Blackberry-Raspberry Dessert

½   cup sugar
¼   cup butter, melted
2   cups graham crackers, crushed
1   3-ounce package raspberry gelatin
1   cup water, boiling
2   cups vanilla ice cream
1   16-ounce can blackberry pie filling
1   tablespoon lemon juice

Assemble ingredients and utensils. In a mixing bowl, combine sugar, butter, and graham cracker crumbs, reserving ¼ cup crumb mixture. Press remaining crumb mixture against bottom of 8-inch square pan. In a saucepan, dissolve gelatin in boiling water; add ice cream and stir to melt ice cream. Chill until thickened. Fold in pie filling and lemon juice. Turn into crumb-lined pan; top with reserved crumbs. Chill until firm. Yield: 8 to 9 servings.

HELPFUL HINT

For a delightful variation, reduce 2 cups graham cracker crumbs to 1¾ cup crumbs and add ¼ cup coconut flakes.

Blueberry Buckle

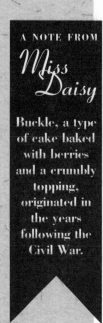
2   cups all-purpose flour, sifted
1   tablespoon baking powder
¼   teaspoon salt
4   tablespoons butter, softened
½   cup sugar
1   egg, lightly beaten
1   teaspoon lemon zest, grated
1   teaspoon vanilla
⅔   cup whole milk
2   cups fresh blueberries (may use frozen)
      confectioners' sugar for garnish

Assemble ingredients and utensils. In a small bowl, combine sifted flour, baking powder, and salt. In the bowl of a food processor (if not available, heavy duty mixer), process butter and sugar until light and fluffy. Add egg and lemon zest. Combine vanilla and milk in a small cup, and alternating with dry ingredients, add milk mixture through the tube of the processor (or slowly by cup into bowl mixture). This will make a very thick batter. Stir in ½ cup berries. Scrape mixture into a buttered 8x8-inch ovenproof glass baking dish. Distribute remaining berries over the surface. Top blueberry batter with streusel topping. Bake in a preheated 350° oven for 45 to 60 minutes, or until the center is cooked through. Cool on wire rack. Sprinkle with confectioners' sugar. Serve warm from the pan. Yield: 6 servings.

Streusel Topping

¼   cup light brown sugar
3   tablespoons all-purpose flour
½   teaspoon ground cinnamon
¼   teaspoon ground ginger
¼   teaspoon ground nutmeg
3   tablespoons soft butter, cut into small pieces

Assemble ingredients and utensils. In a small bowl, combine all dry ingredients, add butter and combine with wooden spoon or fork until butter is absorbed.

~

Quick Cherries Jubilee

Nut Crust
    1   cup butter
    2   cups all-purpose flour
    1   cup pecans, ground

Assemble ingredients and utensils. In a large bowl, combine
all ingredients and pat into a 9x13-inch pan. Bake in a
preheated 400° oven for 20 minutes. Cool.

Filling
    1   8-ounce package cream cheese
    1   16-ounce box confectioners' sugar
    1   16-ounce carton whipped topping or
         1 pint heavy cream, whipped
    1   16-ounce can cherry pie filling

Assemble ingredients and utensils. In a small bowl, combine
cream cheese and sugar. Spread cheese mixture over cooled
nut crust; add whipped topping or whipped heavy cream on
top. Refrigerate. When ready to serve, add cherry pie filling.
Yield: 8 to 9 servings.

Cherry Dumplings

    1   16-ounce can pitted sour cherries
    1   cup plus 2 teaspoons sugar
    1   cup all-purpose flour
    2   teaspoons baking powder
    ¼   teaspoon salt
    ½   cup whole milk
    ½   pint heavy cream

Assemble ingredients and utensils. In a heavy saucepan, bring
cherries and 1 cup sugar to a boil. In a large bowl, sift flour,
baking powder, and salt; add milk to make a stiff dough.
Drop dough from tablespoon into boiling cherries. Cover
tightly and simmer for 10 minutes. Whip heavy cream with 2
teaspoons sugar; serve over warm dumplings. Yield: 6 to 8
servings.

Lemon Curd

5   egg yolks
1   egg white
¼   cup lemon juice
1   cup sugar
3   tablespoons butter

Assemble ingredients and utensils. In the top of a double boiler, combine all ingredients. Cook until thick and clear, stirring constantly. Store in jar and keep refrigerated for up to 2 weeks. Serve with crumpets, tea cakes, gingerbread; use as a filling; or serve in a dessert dish and garnish with whipped cream and grated lemon zest. Yield: 8 servings.

Mandarin Orange Delight

1   16-ounce can mandarin oranges
1   8-ounce can crushed pineapple
12 large marshmallows
1   6-ounce package orange gelatin
1   8-ounce package cream cheese
½   pint heavy cream, whipped

Assemble ingredients and utensils. Drain oranges and pineapple and set fruit aside; reserve the liquid. Add enough water to reserved fruit liquid to equal 2 cups. In a saucepan, heat liquid and dissolve marshmallows and cream cheese; pour over gelatin in a large bowl. Add 2 cups cold water; mix well. Pour into 9x13-inch pan; refrigerate until slightly congealed. Fold whipped heavy cream, oranges, and pineapple into salad; return pan to refrigerator and allow to congeal for serving. Yield: 6 to 9 servings.

Peach Bavarian with Raspberry Sauce

2   eggs, separated
1   3-ounce package peach gelatin
⅛   teaspoon salt
1   cup water, boiling
¼   teaspoon vanilla
¼   teaspoon almond extract
2   tablespoons sugar
1   cup diced peaches, drained
1   cup heavy cream, whipped

Assemble ingredients and utensils. Beat egg yolks; add gelatin and salt. Pour in water and stir until dissolved. Add vanilla and almond extract; set aside. Beat egg whites until stiff, gradually adding sugar. Fold gelatin into egg white mixture. Fold in peaches and whipped heavy cream. Pour into a 6-cup mold and chill until firm. Serve with raspberry sauce. Yield: 6 to 8 servings.

Raspberry Sauce

1   6-ounce package frozen red raspberries
1   teaspoon cornstarch
1   tablespoon water
¼   cup sugar
½   cup red currant jelly
1   tablespoon all-purpose flour
¼   cup cherry brandy or triple sec

Assemble ingredients and utensils. Thaw berries, heat, and strain through a sieve. Mix cornstarch and water; combine with strained berries in a saucepan. Cook and stir for 5 minutes. Add sugar and jelly and heat until fully dissolved. Add flour and triple sec. Stir until well blended. Chill. Serve over fresh sliced peaches, cantaloupe, ice cream, cake, or Peach Bavarian.

Peach Melba

½ cup sugar
1 cup water
3 peaches, peeled, pitted, and halved
   juice of ½ a lemon
   Homemade Vanilla Ice Cream (see p. 64)

Assemble ingredients and utensils. In a heavy saucepan, combine sugar with 1 cup water and boil for 2 minutes. Add peaches; cover and poach for 10 to 15 minutes. Drain, sprinkle with lemon juice, and chill. To serve, place a scoop of vanilla ice cream in each peach half and top with melba sauce. Yield: 6 servings.

Melba Sauce

1 10-ounce package frozen raspberries
¾ cup black currant jelly
¼ cup sugar
½ teaspoon lemon juice

Assemble ingredients and utensils. Cook first 3 ingredients over medium heat, stirring until mixture comes to a boil. Simmer, stirring occasionally, for 20 minutes. Strain and cool. Add lemon juice. Chill. Yield: 2½ cups.

To peel and pit peaches, immerse peaches in boiling water for 10 to 20 seconds, then run a knife along the indentation of the peach. Remove the skin. Twist the halves to free the stone. Freestone peaches are easiest to pit.

A TIP FROM

Miss Daisy

Peaches with Sherry Sauce

10   peaches, peeled, pitted, and halved
3   tablespoons butter
2–3   tablespoons sugar
10–12   macaroons, crumbled (see p. 19)

Assemble ingredients and utensils. Place peaches in baking dish, cut sides up. Place 1 teaspoon of butter into each hollow; sprinkle lightly with sugar. Sprinkle with crumbs, pressing them lightly into the butter. Bake in a preheated 350° oven for 30 minutes. Serve bubbling hot with sherry sauce. Yield: 10 servings.

Sherry Sauce

6   egg yolks
3   tablespoons sugar
2/3   cup dry sherry

Assemble ingredients and utensils. Beat egg yolks and sugar in the top of a double boiler until light and fluffy. Gradually add sherry. Cook, whisking constantly, until smooth and thickened. Chill thoroughly. Yield: 6 servings.

~

Dessert Pears

2   tablespoons butter, melted
1/3   cup light brown sugar
1/2   teaspoon ground cinnamon
1/4   teaspoon ground ginger
1   29-ounce can pear halves, drained
Homemade Vanilla Ice Cream (see p. 64)

Assemble ingredients and utensils. In a heavy saucepan, simmer first five ingredients for 10 minutes, turning pears once. Spoon ice cream into favorite dessert dishes or stemware; top with hot pears and liquid; serve immediately. Yield: 6 servings.

Pineapple Delight

1   3-ounce package orange gelatin
1⅓ cups hot water
4   ounces cream cheese, softened
1   8¼-ounce can crushed pineapple (with juice)
¾   cup sweetened flaked coconut
    whipped cream or sour cream, and fresh
      strawberries for garnish

Assemble ingredients and utensils. In a saucepan, dissolve gelatin in hot water; add cream cheese. Whip until blended and fluffy. Stir in pineapple with juice and coconut. Pour into greased 1-quart mold or greased 1-quart square pan. Chill until firm. Top with whipped cream or sour cream, and fresh strawberries. Yield: 4 to 6 servings.

~

Strawberry Chiffon Squares

⅓   cup butter
1½ cups vanilla wafers, finely crushed
1   3-ounce package strawberry gelatin
¾   cup water, boiling
1   14-ounce can sweetened condensed milk
1   10-ounce package frozen sliced strawberries in
      syrup, thawed
½   pint heavy cream, whipped
4   cups miniature marshmallows
    whipped cream and strawberries for garnish

Assemble ingredients and utensils. In a small saucepan, melt butter; stir in crumbs. Pat crumb mixture firmly into bottom of 11x7-inch baking dish; chill. In a saucepan with boiling water, dissolve gelatin; stir in sweetened condensed milk and undrained strawberries. Fold in whipped heavy cream and marshmallows. Pour into pan; chill 2 hours or until set. Garnish with additional whipped cream and strawberries. Yield: 6 to 8 servings.

Miss Daisy's Trifle

1½ quarts whole milk
1½ cups sugar
2   tablespoons cornstarch
6   eggs
½   cup sherry
2   cups heavy cream
½   of Miss Daisy's Five-Flavor Pound Cake, sliced
     (see p. 121) or ¾ of Miss Daisy's Angel
     Food Cake (see p. 92)
     raspberry or strawberry preserves

Assemble ingredients and utensils. Pour milk into top of a
double boiler. Combine the sugar, cornstarch, and eggs until
smooth; add to the milk; heat until mixture is thickened,
stirring constantly. Set aside to cool. Add sherry to the
cooled custard. Whip the heavy cream and set aside.
Arrange cake slices in a deep glass trifle dish. Spread with
preserves, then top with a layer of custard and a layer of
whipped cream. Repeat until all ingredients are used. Chill.
Yield: 6 to 8 servings.

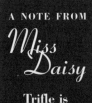

A NOTE FROM

Miss Daisy

Trifle is
originally from
England. The
dessert consists
of sponge cake
or ladyfingers
doused with
spirits (usually
sherry),
covered with
jam or custard,
and topped
with whipped
cream.

Fresh Fruit Pizza

1   20-ounce roll refrigerated sugar cookie dough
1   8-ounce package cream cheese, softened
⅓   cup sugar
1   teaspoon vanilla
2   cups assorted fresh fruit (strawberries, kiwi,
      peaches, blueberries, blackberries)
1   10-ounce jar peach jelly

Assemble ingredients and utensils. Cut cookie dough into
⅛-inch slices; seal edges together to make a crust in a round
pizza pan or jelly roll pan (dough will expand when baked, so
leave a little space at edge of pan). Bake until light brown, 10
to 12 minutes, and cool. In the large bowl of a mixer, combine
cream cheese, sugar, and vanilla; mix until smooth; spread
over cooled crust. Arrange fruit on top of cream cheese
mixture. Heat jelly until slightly runny and carefully spoon
over the fruit to glaze it. Refrigerate until ready to serve.
Yield: 10 to 12 servings.

Berry Sorbet

1 pound fresh cranberries
3 cups water, boiling
1 tablespoon gelatin
½ cup cold water
2 cups sugar
⅛ teaspoon salt
1¼ cups orange juice
1 tablespoon lemon juice

Assemble ingredients and utensils. Bring berries to a boil in the water; cook until soft. Drain and puree. Soften gelatin in cold water for 5 minutes. Combine puree, sugar, salt, and juices in a large saucepan; bring to a boil. Stir in gelatin; blend until completely dissolved. Cool. Freeze until almost firm. Beat until light and fluffy. Freeze again until firm. Yield: 10 servings.

~

Strawberry Sherbet

3 pints fresh strawberries
2 cups sugar
juice of 3 oranges
juice of 3 lemons
⅓ cup triple sec (or favorite liqueur)
1 cup heavy cream, whipped
fresh strawberries or favorite cookie for garnish

Assemble ingredients and utensils. Wash and clean strawberries; remove stems. In a medium bowl, combine strawberries, sugar, orange juice, and lemon juice; let stand for 2 to 3 hours. Mix in blender or food processor until smooth. Stir in triple sec or liqueur. Gently fold in whipped heavy cream. Pour into 2 shallow glass dishes and freeze until solid 1 inch from the side. Return to mixing bowl; beat until mushy. Return to glass dishes and freeze until firm. Serve in sherbet glasses, topped with fresh strawberries or your favorite cookie. Yield: 12 servings.

Tropical Sherbet

      juice of 6 oranges
      juice of 6 lemons
5   medium-ripe bananas, mashed
6   cups water
4   cups sugar
1   quart half-and-half

Assemble ingredients and utensils. Combine all ingredients. Freeze according to ice cream freezer directions. Yield: 2½ to 3 quarts.

Creamy Lemon Ice Cream

5⅓   cups heavy cream
5⅓   cups whole milk
      juice of 8 lemons
4   cups sugar
2   teaspoons lemon extract
1   tablespoon lemon zest, grated

Assemble ingredients and utensils. Combine ingredients. Freeze according to ice cream freezer directions. Yield: 1 gallon.

HELPFUL HINT

This is wonderful served on top of fudge desserts (such as Fudge Cake, p. 107) or fruit desserts.

Peach-of-a-Cream Ice Cream

6   cups mashed ripe peaches
2½   cups sugar
3   eggs
2   tablespoons all-purpose flour
½   teaspoon salt
4   cups whole milk
1   cup heavy cream, whipped
1   tablespoon vanilla

Assemble ingredients and utensils. In a large bowl, combine peaches and 1 cup sugar; stir well and set aside. In the large bowl of a mixer, beat eggs until frothy and light. In a separate bowl, combine 1½ cups sugar, flour, and salt; stir well. Gradually add sugar mixture to egg mixture, beating until thick; add milk and mix well. Pour egg mixture into heavy saucepan; cook over low heat, stirring constantly for about 15 minutes until mixture coats spoon. Remove from heat and cool. Stir in whipped heavy cream and vanilla. Add peaches, stirring well. Pour mixture into chilled freezer can and freeze according to manufacturer's instructions. Let sit for 30 minutes before serving. Yield: 1 gallon.

Homemade Vanilla Ice Cream

2   cups sugar
3   tablespoons cornstarch
¼   teaspoon salt
3   cups half-and-half
4   eggs, lightly beaten
4   cups heavy cream, chilled
2   tablespoons vanilla

Assemble ingredients and utensils. Combine first 3 ingredients in the top of a double boiler and stir in half-and-half. Cook, stirring constantly, until mixture thickens. Add a small amount of hot mixture to eggs, stirring constantly. Stir eggs into hot mixture in double boiler and continue cooking for 5 to 6 minutes, stirring constantly. Remove from heat and cool slightly. Stir in heavy cream and vanilla. Refrigerate until freezing time. Freeze in an electric or hand crank freezer according to freezer directions. Yield: 3 quarts.

~

Blueberry Ice Cream

1   envelope unflavored gelatin
½   cup whole milk, cold
½   cup whole milk, heated to boiling
2   cups fresh blueberries
¾   cup sugar
2   cups heavy cream, whipped

Assemble ingredients and utensils. In a 5-cup blender, sprinkle unflavored gelatin over cold milk; set aside 3 to 4 minutes. Add hot milk and process at low speed until gelatin is completely dissolved, about 2 minutes. Cool completely. Add blueberries and sugar; process at high speed until blended. Pour into large bowl and chill, stirring occasionally, until mixture mounds slightly when dropped from spoon. Fold whipped heavy cream into gelatin mixture. Pour into two 4x10-inch freezer trays or one 8-inch baking pan; freeze until firm. Yield: 1½ quarts ice cream.

Coffee Marshmallow Ice Cream

¾   pound marshmallows
¼   cup sugar
3   cups brewed coffee, hot
2   cups heavy cream
1   cup half-and-half
1½ teaspoons vanilla
¼   teaspoon salt

Assemble ingredients and utensils. In a mixing bowl, add marshmallows and sugar to hot coffee; mix well; chill thoroughly. Add heavy cream, half-and-half, vanilla, and salt. Freeze according to ice cream freezer directions. Yield: 3 quarts.

Peppermint Stick Ice Cream

4   cups whole milk
1   pound peppermint candy, crushed
2   tablespoons all-purpose flour
½   cup sugar
⅓   teaspoon salt
2   egg yolks, beaten
8   cups heavy cream

Assemble ingredients and utensils. In a heavy saucepan, heat milk and candy to boiling point. In a small bowl, combine flour, sugar, salt, and beaten egg yolks; add to milk and candy mixture; cook until thick. Cool. Add heavy cream. Freeze according to ice cream freezer directions. Yield: 1 gallon.

A TIP FROM

Miss Daisy

If you don't have a sauce made, try these ideas:

- Soften coffee ice cream with dark rum and serve over vanilla ice cream, garnished with shaved chocolate.
- Mix vanilla ice cream with fresh or frozen berries, cherries, or peaches to the consistency of whipped cream and serve over fresh fruit.

Chocolate Rum Ice Cream

¼	cup sugar
⅓	cup water
2	tablespoons strong brewed coffee
1	6-ounce package semi-sweet chocolate chips
3	egg yolks
2	ounces dark rum
1½	cups heavy cream, whipped
½	cup slivered almonds, toasted

Assemble ingredients and utensils. In a small saucepan, place sugar, water, and brewed coffee. Bring to boil, stirring constantly; cook for 1 minute. In a food processor or blender, add chocolate chips; with motor running, pour hot syrup over and blend until smooth. Blend in egg yolks and rum; cool slightly. Fold chocolate mixture into bowl of whipped heavy cream. Pour into individual serving dishes and sprinkle with toasted almonds. Freeze. Remove from freezer at least 5 minutes before serving. Yield: 6 servings.

~

Eggnog Frozen Dessert

1	cup sugar
⅓	cup water
⅛	teaspoon cream of tartar
4	egg yolks
⅛	teaspoon salt
3	tablespoons dark rum
3	cups heavy cream, whipped

Assemble ingredients and utensils. In a heavy saucepan, combine sugar, water, and cream of tartar. Bring to a boil and cook to 136°F, testing with a candy thermometer. In a blender, add egg yolks, salt, and rum; cover and blend on high. Remove cover and with motor on low, gradually pour in the hot syrup; turn off motor. Chill mixture until thick. Fold mixture into the whipped heavy cream. Turn mixture into a 6-cup mold or into 18 small greased or paper-lined muffin tins. Freeze. Yield: 18 individual servings or 1 6-cup mold.

Ice Cream Cookie Pie

2   cups chocolate sandwich cookies, crushed
¼   cup butter, melted
1   5-ounce can evaporated milk
2   tablespoons butter
½   cup sugar
2   ounces semi-sweet chocolate
½   teaspoon vanilla
1   quart vanilla ice cream, softened
1   8-ounce container whipped topping
      chocolate shavings for garnish

Assemble ingredients and utensils. In a bowl, combine cookie crumbs and melted butter; divide and press into 2 8-inch pie plates. In a saucepan, heat milk, butter, sugar, and chocolate; stir until thickened. Remove from heat. Add vanilla; stir and let cool. Spread softened ice cream over crust. Spoon the chocolate sauce over ice cream. Place the pie in the freezer until ready to serve. Remove and frost with whipped topping. Garnish with chocolate shavings. Yield: 2 8-inch pies.

Favorite Mud Pie

21   chocolate sandwich cookies, crushed
6   tablespoons butter, melted
1   quart chocolate ice cream, softened
4   tablespoons brewed coffee, cold
2   tablespoons brandy
2   tablespoons coffee liqueur
1   cup heavy cream, whipped
1   12-ounce jar fudge sauce (or your favorite
      homemade)
      toasted almonds and cherries to garnish

Assemble ingredients and utensils. Mix cookie crumbs with butter. Press into 9- or 10-inch pie pan. Freeze. Whip ice cream with coffee, brandy, and liqueur. Add 4 tablespoons whipped heavy cream to ice cream mixture and continue to whip. Spread in frozen pie shell. Freeze until very hard. Dip knife in hot water; working quickly, spread room temperature fudge sauce on top of frozen pie. Cover with remaining whipped heavy cream. Garnish with toasted almonds and cherries. Freeze. Yield: 8 servings.

A TIP FROM

Miss Daisy

Other garnishing ideas include shaved semi-sweet or sweetened chocolate, grated orange or lemon zest, nuts, coconut, or fresh fruit.

Banana Split Dessert

1 cup milk chocolate chips
½ cup butter
2 cups confectioners' sugar
1½ cups whole milk
1 teaspoon vanilla
1½–2 cups graham crackers, crushed
5 bananas, sliced
½ gallon ice cream (Neapolitan or any other flavor)
1 cup heavy cream, whipped
  chopped nuts for garnish

Assemble ingredients and utensils. In a heavy saucepan, melt together chocolate chips and butter; add sugar and milk. Cook at a heavy boil for 8 minutes or until thick, stirring constantly. Add vanilla and cool. Cover bottom of 9x13-inch pan with graham cracker crumbs. Cover with sliced bananas. Slice ice cream and place over bananas. Cover with cooled chocolate sauce. Freeze. Serve with whipped heavy cream and sprinkle nuts on top. Yield: 12 to 16 servings.

Rum Tortoni

½ cup almonds, minced
½ cup sweetened flaked coconut, toasted
½ cup seedless dark raisins
4 cups vanilla ice cream and 1 tablespoon rum
      extract or 4 cups rum raisin ice cream and
      1 teaspoon rum extract
  maraschino cherries
  whipped cream and stemmed cherries for garnish

Assemble ingredients and utensils. In a small bowl, combine almonds, coconut, and raisins. In a medium bowl, soften ice cream until thin, but not runny; quickly stir in rum extract and almond mixture. Spoon into greased or paper-lined 2½-inch muffin tins. Freeze slightly and top with maraschino cherries. Freeze until firm. Remove from freezer just before serving. Serve with dollop of whipped cream and a stemmed cherry on top. Yield: 12 to 14 servings.

Chocolate Ice Box Dessert

4   1-ounce squares semi-sweet chocolate
1   cup butter, softened
    pinch of salt
1   cup sugar or 2 cups confectioners' sugar
6   eggs, separated
18 lady fingers
18 macaroons (see p. 19)
    whipped cream for garnish

Assemble ingredients and utensils. In a heavy saucepan, melt
chocolate. In the large bowl of a mixer, beat butter and blend
into chocolate. Add pinch of salt. Beat sugar into egg yolks.
Stir into chocolate mixture. Whip egg whites and fold into
mixture. Pour into bowl lined with lady fingers. Crush macaroons and sprinkle on top. Store in refrigerator and serve with
whipped cream. Yield: 8 servings.

Chocolate Mint Dessert

Crust
25 chocolate wafer cookies, crushed
¼   cup butter, melted
½   gallon peppermint ice cream

Assemble ingredients and utensils. In a large bowl, combine
crushed cookies and melted butter; press into 9x13-inch
pan. Spread slightly softened ice cream on chocolate cookie
crust and freeze.

Sauce
3   1-ounce squares unsweetened baking chocolate
¼   cup butter
¾   cup sugar
1   5-ounce can evaporated milk
    whipped cream, fresh mint, and a fresh raspberry
        for garnish

A TIP FROM

Miss Daisy

If your store-
bought ice
cream is hard
and won't
spoon, peel off
the carton and
slice with a
cake knife.

Assemble ingredients and utensils. In a medium saucepan,
combine first 4 ingredients. Cook over medium heat, stirring
constantly, until chocolate is melted, about 4 or 5 minutes.
Remove from heat and cool completely. Spread over frozen
ice cream mixture and return to freezer. Cut into squares to
serve and top with whipped cream, fresh mint, and a fresh
raspberry. Yield: 12 to 16 servings.

Frozen Mocha Torte

1   cup crisp macaroon cookie crumbs (see
        Macaroons, p. 19)
2–3   tablespoons butter, melted
3   cups chocolate ice cream, softened
½   cup hot fudge sauce, cooled
3   cups coffee ice cream, softened
4   ounces chocolate-coated toffee candy bars,
        coarsely crushed

Assemble ingredients and utensils. In a small bowl, stir together cookie crumbs and butter; lightly press onto bottom of 9- or 10-inch springform pan. Bake in a preheated 350° oven for 7 to 10 minutes, or until lightly browned; cool. Spread chocolate ice cream evenly over cooled crust. Drizzle with ¼ cup hot fudge sauce; freeze until firm. Top with layer of coffee ice cream; sprinkle evenly with crushed candy; and drizzle with remaining ¼ cup hot fudge sauce. Cover; freeze until firm. Yield: 10 to 12 servings.

Frozen Pumpkin Squares

¼   pound marshmallows, chopped
1   cup pumpkin, cooked or canned
¼   teaspoon ground cinnamon
⅛   teaspoon ground nutmeg
⅛   teaspoon ground ginger
⅛   teaspoon salt
1   pint Homemade Vanilla Ice Cream (see p. 64)
        ginger cookies, crumbled
        whipped cream or sour cream, and mandarin
        oranges for garnish

Assemble ingredients and utensils. In the top of a double boiler, place marshmallows, pumpkin, cinnamon, nutmeg, ginger, and salt. Heat, stirring occasionally, until marshmallows are melted. Cool slightly; stir in ice cream. Line 9x9-inch pan or refrigerator tray with cookie crumbs, reserving one fourth of crumbs for top. Pour pumpkin mixture over crumbs, sprinkle remaining crumbs on top. Freeze. Remove from freezer 10 minutes before serving. Cut in squares; top with whipped cream or sour cream and a mandarin orange slice. Yield: 8 servings.

Frozen Stawberry Mousse

1 16-ounce box frozen strawberries
2 cups sour cream
1 cup sugar
1 tablespoon plus 1 teaspoon vanilla
   whipped cream and fresh whole strawberries for
   garnish

Assemble ingredients and utensils. Thaw strawberries; combine with remaining ingredients; beat well. Pour into 2 freezer trays or glass dish. Cover with foil; freeze. Allow to thaw for 10 minutes before serving. Cut in squares or scoop out and serve in sherbet dishes. Garnish with whipped cream and a fresh strawberry on top. Yield: 8 servings.

Pink Arctic Freeze

1 8-ounce package cream cheese, softened
2 tablespoons mayonnaise
2 tablespoons sugar
1 16-ounce can whole berry cranberry sauce
1 cup crushed pineapple, drained
1 cup heavy cream, whipped
   whipped cream for garnish
   fresh raspberries or fresh mint for garnish

Assemble ingredients and utensils. In the large bowl of a mixer, beat together cream cheese, mayonnaise, and sugar. Add cranberry sauce and drained pineapple; mix well. Fold in whipped heavy cream. Freeze in 9x9-inch dish. Cut into squares to serve; garnish with dollop of whipped cream and fresh raspberries or fresh mint. Yield: 6 to 9 servings.

HELPFUL HINT

This is also wonderful as a salad!

Raspberry Bombe

6 cups red raspberry sherbet
4 cups peppermint ice cream
1 cup heavy cream
3 tablespoons confectioners' sugar
⅛ teaspoon salt
¼ cup mixed candied fruits (maraschino cherries, pineapple, etc.)
¼ cup toasted almonds, chopped
¾ teaspoon rum flavoring

Assemble ingredients and utensils. Chill 2½-quart mold (or bowl) in freezer. In a medium bowl, stir sherbet just to soften; spread a layer over bottom and side of mold; freeze until firm. In a second medium bowl, stir ice cream until soft; spread quickly over sherbet layer; freeze until firm. In a third medium bowl, whip heavy cream with sugar and salt; gently fold in fruits and almonds; add rum flavoring. Pile into center of mold; smooth top. Cover with foil and freeze overnight. To quickly loosen ice cream from mold, immerse in pan of hot water; peel off foil; invert onto chilled plate. Yield: 6 to 8 servings.

A bombe is a sophisticated French dessert that contains different flavors of ice cream and sherbet and is frozen into a mold. When you prepare Raspberry Bombe, or any frozen or chilled dessert in a mold pan or dish, grease the pan with a bit of mayonnaise to help it come out quickly and easily.

A TIP FROM

Miss Daisy

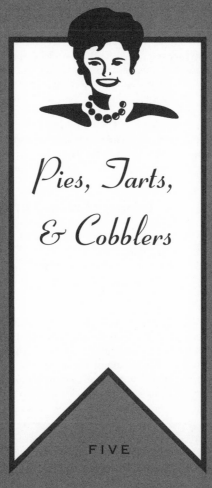

Pies, Tarts,
& Cobblers

FIVE

Pie Crust

HELPFUL
HINT

Handle pie
dough very
little after
adding water.
Excess
handling
results in a
tough crust
that is not
flaky.

1½   cups all-purpose flour, sifted
½   teaspoon salt
½   cup shortening
3   tablespoons water

Assemble ingredients and utensils. In a mixing bowl, sift flour and salt; cut in shortening with pastry blender or 2 knives until the mixture resembles coarse cornmeal. Sprinkle with water, 1 teaspoon at a time; mix thoroughly with a fork. When all of the flour is moistened, gather the dough into a ball. Roll out the dough into a circle about ⅛-inch thick and about 1½ inches larger than the pie plate. Turn into pie plate; trim excess dough from rim of pie plate. Chill until ready to use. For a prebaked pie crust, prick shell close and deep on bottom and sides. Bake in a preheated 450° oven for 12 to 15 minutes or until golden brown. Yield: Enough for one 9-inch or 10-inch single-crust pie.

Graham Cracker Crust

HELPFUL
HINT

You will need
18 to 20
graham
crackers to
equal 1½
cups,
crushed.

1½   cups graham crackers, crushed
⅓   cup sugar
¾   teaspoon ground cinnamon
⅛   teaspoon ground nutmeg
½   cup butter, melted

Assemble ingredients and utensils. In a medium bowl, combine graham cracker crumbs, sugar, cinnamon, and nutmeg; add butter and blend thoroughly. Pack evenly over bottom and sides of 9-inch pie plate, making a standing rim. Bake in a preheated 350° oven for 5 minutes. Chill. Fill with desired filling and bake for another 7 to 8 minutes. Yield: 1 9-inch pie crust.

Use a pastry cloth over a rolling pin when rolling the crust. You will use less flour, fewer strokes, and have a tender, flakier crust. Never wash a rolling pin or pastry board. Simply scrape it with a knife. Washing makes it stick the next time around.

A TIP FROM
Miss Daisy

Lattice Cherry Pie

⅔ cup sugar
2   tablespoons cornstarch
⅛ teaspoon salt
¾ cup cherry juice (drained from frozen cherries)
⅛ teaspoon almond extract
3   drops red food coloring
2   tablespoons butter
2   cups frozen cherries, thawed and drained
      (reserve the juice)
      whipped cream (optional)

Assemble ingredients and utensils. In a heavy saucepan, mix together sugar, cornstarch, and salt; gradually add in the cherry juice. Cook until mixture is thick and clear. Remove from heat and add almond extract, red food coloring, butter, and cherries. Let cool while preparing crust.

Woven Lattice Crust

2   cups all-purpose flour
1   teaspoon salt
¾ vegetable shortening
⅓ cup whole milk

Assemble ingredients and utensils. In a mixing bowl, sift flour and add salt. Blend in shortening with pastry blender or 2 knives until mixture is about the size of large peas. Stir in milk. Press into a ball and divide in half, one ball slightly larger than the other. Place larger ball on the floured pastry cloth or a wooden counter, and roll out bottom crust for a 9-inch pie. Fit into 9-inch pie pan. Roll out other ball of dough and cut into strips about ½-inch wide. Pour filling into pie crust, weave lattice on top of filling and flute edge. Bake in a preheated 400° oven for 45 minutes until golden brown. Delicious topped with whipped cream. Yield: 6 to 8 servings.

A TIP FROM

Miss Daisy

When baking fruit pies, place a sheet of aluminum foil directly under the pie plate on the bottom of the oven to catch the drippings from the pie.

A TIP FROM
Miss Daisy

Cream Cheese Pie with Blackberries and Peaches

Crust

½   cup unsalted butter, melted
½   teaspoon almond extract
2½ cups Shortbread Wedge cookies, crumbled
(see p. 17)

Assemble ingredients and utensils. In a medium bowl, combine butter and almond extract; mix in crumbs. Press crumb mixture over bottom and sides of 10-inch pie dish. Bake in a preheated 325° oven for 7 to 8 minutes. Cool crust completely.

Filling and Topping

1   8-ounce package cream cheese, softened
¾   cup confectioners' sugar
½   cup heavy cream
1   teaspoon vanilla
¾   teaspoon almond extract
3   large peaches, peeled, pitted, and sliced
1   pint fresh blackberries
¼   cup peach jam, melted

Assemble ingredients and utensils. In a food processor or blender, mix cream cheese until smooth; add sugar, heavy cream, vanilla, and almond extract; blend until very smooth. Spread filling in prepared cooled crust; refrigerate until filling is firm. Arrange peach slices around edge of pie; arrange blackberries in center. Brush warm jam lightly over fruit to glaze. Refrigerate several hours before serving. Yield: 6 to 8 servings.

Triple Fruit Pie

1 ¼   cups each of fresh blueberries, raspberries, and chopped rhubarb
½   teaspoon almond extract
1 ¼   cups sugar
¼   cup quick-cooking tapioca
¼   teaspoon ground nutmeg
¼   teaspoon salt
1   tablespoon lemon juice
      woven lattice crust (see p. 75)

(see p. 75)

Assemble ingredients and utensils. In a large bowl, combine fruits and extract; toss to coat. In another bowl, combine sugar, tapioca, nutmeg, and salt; add to fruit; stir gently. Let stand for 15 minutes. Line 9-inch pie plate with bottom crust; trim pastry even with edge. Stir lemon juice into fruit mixture; spoon into the crust. Roll out remaining pastry; make a lattice crust; seal and flute edges. Bake in a preheated 400° oven for 20 minutes; reduce the heat to 350° and bake 30 minutes longer, or until the crust is golden brown and the filling is bubbly. Yield: 6 to 8 servings.

Apple Ribbon Pie

6–8   tart apples
      woven lattice crust (see p. 75)
1   cup sugar
1   tablespoon all-purpose flour
¼   teaspoon ground nutmeg
½   teaspoon ground cinnamon
2   tablespoons butter or margarine
¼   cup sharp cheddar cheese, grated
1 ½   teaspoons poppy seeds

(see p. 75)

Assemble ingredients and utensils. Pare and core apples; thinly slice. Line 9-inch pie pan with pastry. In a medium bowl, combine sugar, flour, and spices; rub a little of this mixture into pastry in pie pan. Fill pie pan with sliced apples; add remaining sugar mixture. Dot with butter or margarine. Divide remaining pastry into two equal portions. Roll out 1 portion ⅛-inch thick; top with grated cheese; fold over in 3 layers; roll out again. Cut into 5 strips 10 inches long by ¾-inch wide. Repeat with remaining portion of pastry, using poppy seed instead of cheese. Weave strips, lattice fashion, on pie, alternating cheese strips and poppy seed strips; trim and flute edge. Bake in a preheated 425° oven for 40 to 45 minutes, or until apples are tender. Yield: 6 to 8 servings.

HELPFUL HINT

Roll out pie dough between 2 sheets of waxed paper. Peel one sheet of paper off, turn the dough upside down in the pie shell, and carefully peel off the other sheet of paper.

HELPFUL HINT

To prevent juices in berry pies from running over, stick a few pieces of uncooked pasta (such as macaroni or penne pasta) through the top of the crust.

Apple Cream Pie

HELPFUL HINT

You can keep pie dough in the refrigerator for 3 to 4 days or in the freezer for 5 to 6 months. Thaw the frozen dough in the refrigerator and then let stand at room temperature for 30 minutes before rolling it out.

3   cups tart apples, chopped
½   cup sugar
1   tablespoon all-purpose flour
¼   teaspoon mace
1   9-inch unbaked pie crust (see p. 74)
2   tablespoons butter

Assemble ingredients and utensils. Combine apples, sugar, flour, and mace. Spread apple mixture in pie crust. Dot with butter and bake in a preheated 450° oven for 10 minutes. Reduce temperature to 350° and bake 35 minutes longer or until apples are tender. Cool; spread with cream filling.

Cream Filling

1½ cups whole milk
¼   cup sugar
¼   teaspoon salt
3   tablespoons all-purpose flour
1   egg, beaten
1   tablespoon butter
½   teaspoon vanilla

Assemble ingredients and utensils. In the top of a double boiler, scald 1 cup milk. Mix sugar, salt, flour, and remaining milk together. Stir into hot milk. Cover and cook slowly for 4 minutes or until thickened, stirring constantly. Add egg slowly to mixture and cook 1 minute longer. Add butter and vanilla. Pour over apples in pie crust. Yield: 6 to 8 servings.

Coconut Cream Pie

⅔ cup sugar
¼ cup cornstarch
½ teaspoon salt
3 cups whole milk
4 egg yolks, beaten
2 tablespoons butter
4 teaspoons vanilla
1 3½-ounce can sweetened flaked coconut
1 10-inch pie crust, baked and cooled (see p. 74)
½ cup heavy cream, whipped

Assemble ingredients and utensils. In a saucepan, combine sugar, cornstarch, and salt. Combine milk and egg yolks and gradually stir into sugar mixture. Cook over medium heat, stirring constantly until mixture thickens and comes to a boil. Boil and stir for 1 minute. Remove from heat and blend in butter and vanilla. Add three-fourths can of coconut. Pour into pie crust. Refrigerate. Before serving, top with whipped heavy cream (you may sweeten this to taste) and sprinkle with remaining coconut. Yield: 6 to 8 servings.

French Coconut Pie

3 eggs, beaten
¼ teaspoon salt
1 teaspoon vanilla
¼ teaspoon almond extract
¼ teaspoon coconut extract
1½ cups sugar
2 tablespoons all-purpose flour
1 tablespoon apple cider vinegar
½ cup butter, melted
1 cup sweetened flaked coconut
1 9-inch unbaked pie crust (see p. 74)

Assemble ingredients and utensils. In the large bowl of a mixer, blend eggs, salt, vanilla, and almond and coconut extracts. Combine sugar and flour and stir into egg mixture. Add vinegar. Stir in melted butter. Mix well. Fold in coconut. Pour into unbaked pie crust. Bake in a preheated 300° oven for 1 hour. Yield: 6 to 8 servings.

HELPFUL HINT

Most pies should be stored at room temperature, loosely covered with aluminum foil to keep them crisp. Store custard and cream pies in the refrigerator, but let them warm to room temperature before serving.

Thanksgiving Pumpkin Pie

1½ cups canned or fresh cooked pumpkin, mashed
¾ cup sugar
½ teaspoon salt
1¼ teaspoons ground cinnamon
1 teaspoon ground ginger
½ teaspoon ground nutmeg
½ teaspoon ground cloves
3 eggs, lightly beaten
1¼ cups whole milk
⅔ cup evaporated milk
1 9-inch unbaked pie crust (see p. 74)

(see p. 74)

Assemble ingredients and utensils. In a large bowl, combine pumpkin, sugar, salt, and spices; blend in eggs, milk, and evaporated milk; mix well. Pour into unbaked pastry shell. This is a very generous filling, so the edges of the pie shell may have to be crimped high so that the batter won't run out. Bake in a preheated 400° oven for about 50 minutes. Yield: 6 to 8 servings.

HELPFUL HINT

To keep the bottom crust of a pie from getting soggy, brush the surface with the well-beaten white of an egg.

Sweet Potato Custard Pie

1½ cups sweet potatoes, cooked and mashed
½ cup dark brown sugar
2 eggs, beaten
½ teaspoon salt
1 teaspoon ground allspice
1½ cups whole milk
1 9-inch unbaked pie crust (see p. 74)

(see p. 74)

Assemble ingredients and utensils. In a large bowl, combine all ingredients. Pour into pie crust and bake in a preheated 350° oven for 20 minutes. Add topping and continue baking for an additional 25 minutes. Yield: 6 to 8 servings.

Topping
4 tablespoons butter, melted
¼ cup dark brown sugar
¾ cup pecans, chopped

Assemble ingredients and utensils. Combine all ingredients. Sprinkle on custard and bake until custard is firm and golden brown, about 25 minutes.

HELPFUL HINT

Start pastry in a hot oven, because the contrast of the heat and the cool dough causes rapid air expansion which contributes to a light, flaky texture.

Miss Daisy's Jackson Pie

1 cup sugar
¼ cup butter, melted
3 eggs, lightly beaten
¾ cup light corn syrup
¼ teaspoon salt
2 tablespoons Jack Daniel's® Tennessee Whiskey
1 teaspoon vanilla
½ cup pecans, chopped
½ cup semi-sweet chocolate chips
1 9-inch unbaked pie crust (see p. 74)

Assemble ingredients and utensils. In the large bowl of a mixer, combine sugar and butter. Add eggs, syrup, salt, Jack Daniel's®, and vanilla. Mix until blended. Spread pecans and chocolate chips evenly in bottom of unbaked pie shell. Pour filling into shell. Bake in a preheated 375° oven for 40 to 50 minutes. Yield: 6 to 8 servings.

~

Quick Chess Pie

2 eggs, beaten
1 cup sugar
½ cup light brown sugar
1 tablespoon white corn meal
1 tablespoon all-purpose flour
¼ cup whole milk
½ cup butter, melted
½ teaspoon apple cider vinegar
1 tablespoon vanilla
1 9-inch unbaked pie crust (see p. 74)

Assemble ingredients and utensils. In the large bowl of a mixer, combine all ingredients and mix for 4 to 5 minutes. Pour into pie crust. Bake in a preheated 325° oven for 35 to 40 minutes. Yield: 6 to 8 servings.

Meringue Topping

4   egg whites
¼   teaspoon cream of tartar
¼   teaspoon lemon extract or ½ teaspoon vanilla
½   cup sugar

Assemble ingredients and utensils. In the large bowl of a
mixer, combine egg whites, cream of tartar, and lemon
extract or vanilla; beat until egg whites are foamy. Add
sugar gradually, 1 tablespoon at a time, and beat until sugar
is dissolved and whites are stiff, glossy, and hold soft peaks.
Spread carefully over hot or warm filling, sealing it securely
to edge of crust. Bake in a preheated 375° oven 12 to 15
minutes, or until meringue is lightly browned.

Chocolate Meringue Pie

3   eggs, separated
1   cup plus 3 tablespoons sugar
1   1-ounce square semi-sweet chocolate
1   tablespoon butter
2   tablespoons all-purpose flour
1   cup whole milk, lukewarm
1   teaspoon vanilla
1   9-inch pie crust, baked (see p. 74)

Assemble ingredients and utensils. Beat egg yolks and 1 cup
sugar together until creamy. In the top of a double boiler, melt
chocolate and butter. Add chocolate mixture and flour to egg
yolk mixture. Add milk and blend well. Blend in vanilla.
Cook mixture in the top of a double boiler until quite thick,
stirring often. Pour thickened chocolate into pie crust. Cover
with meringue made of 3 egg whites stiffly beaten with 3
tablespoons of sugar. Spoon meringue over chocolate,
spreading well to all edges of pie shell. Bake in a preheated
350° oven for 10 to 15 minutes. Yield: One 9-inch pie.

Lemon Meringue Pie

¼ cup cornstarch
3   tablespoons all-purpose flour
1¾ cups sugar
⅛   teaspoon salt
2   cups water
4   egg yolks, lightly beaten (reserving whites for meringue)
½   cup lemon juice
1   tablespoon lemon zest, grated
1   tablespoon butter
1   9-inch pie crust, baked (see p. 74)

Assemble ingredients and utensils. In a heavy saucepan, combine cornstarch, flour, sugar, and salt; mix well. Gradually add water; stir over medium heat until mixture comes to a boil. Boil for 1 minute until shiny and translucent. Quickly add some of hot mixture to egg yolks. Pour yolk mixture back into hot mixture; stir to blend. Return to heat and cook over low heat for 5 minutes, stirring occasionally. Remove from heat; stir in lemon juice, lemon zest, and butter. Pour into prebaked pie shell. Prepare meringue. Spoon meringue over pie; spread evenly and be sure to spread to edges to seal all around. Bake in a preheated 350° oven for 12 to 15 minutes or until the meringue is lightly browned. Cool on rack. Yield: 6 to 8 servings.

Meringue

1   tablespoon cornstarch
½   cup cold water
6   tablespoons sugar
¼   teaspoon salt
4   egg whites (reserved from pie recipe)

Assemble ingredients and utensils. In a saucepan, combine cornstarch, water, 2 tablespoons sugar, and salt. Cook over medium heat stirring constantly until thick and clear. Cool completely. In a separate bowl, beat egg whites until stiff peaks form, gradually adding 4 tablespoons sugar; beat well. Slowly add cooled cornstarch mixture, beating until stiff and glossy.

∼

HELPFUL HINT

Slightly butter or oil your knife first before trying to cut through the meringue. It keeps the meringue in place and prevents it from breaking down or falling.

∼

Miss Daisy's Lemon Ice Box Pie

3   egg yolks
1   14-ounce can sweetened condensed milk
1   teaspoon lemon zest, grated
½   cup fresh squeezed lemon juice
1   9-inch graham cracker crust, baked (see p. 74)
    whipped cream and lemon slices for garnish

Assemble ingredients and utensils. In a mixing bowl, beat the egg yolks until thick and lemon colored; fold in sweetened condensed milk, lemon zest, and juice. Pour mixture into baked pie shell. Bake in a preheated 325° oven for 7 to 10 minutes, until mixture is thickened. Cool to room temperature. Top with whipped cream and a slice of lemon. Yield: 6 to 8 servings.

Miss Daisy's Key Lime Pie

3   egg yolks
1   14-ounce can sweetened condensed milk
1   teaspoon lime zest, grated
½   cup key lime juice
1   9-inch graham cracker crust, baked (see p. 74)
    whipped cream and lime slices for garnish

Assemble ingredients and utensils. In a mixing bowl, beat the egg yolks until thick and lemon colored; fold in sweetened condensed milk, lime zest, and juice. Pour mixture into baked pie shell. Bake in a preheated 325° oven for 7 to 10 minutes, until mixture is thickened. Cool to room temperature. Top with whipped cream and a slice of lime. Yield: 6 to 8 servings.

Lemon Tarts

4　eggs, beaten well
1　cup sugar
¼　cup butter, melted
⅛　teaspoon salt
　　juice and grated zest of 2 large lemons
1　recipe of pie crust (see p. 74)
12　tart tins

Assemble ingredients and utensils. In the large bowl of a mixer, combine eggs, sugar, butter, salt, lemon juice, and zest; mix well. Roll the pie crust dough on a floured surface into a rectangular shape about ¼-inch thick. Space tart tins on dough to determine amount of pastry needed for each. Allow extra amount for each when placing dough in tins—pastry will overflow. Trim to fit tart tin; place in tin and line with foil. Bake in a preheated 425° oven for 10 minutes; remove foil and bake for 5 minutes or until light brown. Fill the baked tart shells with lemon mixture. Bake in a preheated 425° oven for 25 to 30 minutes. Yield: 12 servings.

HELPFUL HINT

Fill pastry-lined tart tins with foil when baking for the first 10 minutes, then remove foil and continue baking until light brown.

Chocolate Tarts

2　1-ounce squares unsweetened chocolate
2　cups whole milk
1　cup sugar
⅓　cup all-purpose flour
½　teaspoon salt
3　egg yolks
1　tablespoon butter
1　teaspoon vanilla
6　tart shells (or 1 recipe of pie crust, see p. 74)

Assemble ingredients and utensils. Melt chocolate and milk over low heat. Add enough milk mixture to make a paste of sugar, flour, and salt. Slowly add this mixture back to chocolate and milk mixture. Cook over low to medium heat until thick, stirring continuously. Beat 3 egg yolks and slowly add to mixture. Cook slowly 1 minute, then add butter and vanilla. Cool. Roll the pie crust dough on a floured surface into a rectangular shape about ¼ -inch thick. Space tart tins on dough to determine amount of pastry needed for each. Trim to fit tart tin; place in tin and line with foil. Bake in a preheated 425° oven for 10 minutes; remove foil and bake for 5 minutes or until light brown. Fill tart shells with cooled chocolate filling. Yield: 6 tarts.

HELPFUL HINT

This recipe also makes a delicious chocolate pie.

Chess Tarts

3   eggs, beaten
1½ cups sugar
1   teaspoon vanilla
6   tablespoons buttermilk
½   cup butter, melted
6–8 tart shells

Assemble ingredients and utensils. In a medium bowl, mix ingredients. Pour into tart shells. Bake in a preheated 350° oven for 30 minutes, then 10 more minutes in a 300° oven until tarts are set. Yield: 6 to 8 servings.

Apple Cranberry Cobbler

4   cups apples, thinly sliced
1   cup cranberries
1   cup sugar
1   teaspoon ground cinnamon
½   teaspoon ground nutmeg
¼   teaspoon salt
½   cup water
2   tablespoons butter, thinly sliced
    baking powder biscuit dough
1   egg, lightly beaten
1   tablespoon water

Assemble ingredients and utensils. Cook apples until just tender in small amount of water; add cranberries; cook 5 minutes longer; drain; pour into shallow baking dish. Blend sugar, spices, salt, water, and butter; pour over apple mixture. Prepare your favorite recipe for baking powder biscuits, using 2 cups flour and adding 2 tablespoons sugar. Or use 2 cups biscuit mix prepared according to package directions, adding 2 tablespoons sugar. Roll out ½-inch thick; cut with round cutter. Cut each round in half, crosswise, and arrange around rim of baking dish with rounded side in. Combine egg and water; brush over biscuits. Bake in a preheated 425° oven for about 25 minutes or until cobbler is bubbly and biscuits are golden brown. May be served plain or with whipped cream or whipped topping. Yield: 8 servings.

Blueberry Mountain Cobbler

½   cup butter
1   cup all-purpose flour
¾   cup sugar
1½ teaspoons baking powder
½   teaspoon salt
¾   cup whole milk
1   pint blueberries
    Ice Cream (optional)

Assemble ingredients and utensils. Melt butter in a 1½-quart glass casserole, set aside. In a large bowl combine flour, half of the ¾ cup sugar, baking powder, and salt, alternately with the milk. Pour over melted butter in casserole. Drop berries and remainder of sugar on top of the batter. Bake in a preheated 325° oven for 1 hour (the berries will sink to the bottom). Yield: 6 servings.

~

A TIP FROM

Miss Daisy

This recipe is delicious when served with ice cream such as Homemade Vanilla Ice Cream.
(see p. 64)

Blackberry Cobbler

1   cup all-purpose flour
1   cup sugar
¼   teaspoon salt
2   teaspoons baking powder
¾   cup whole milk
½   cup melted butter
⅛   teaspoon almond extract
2   cups fresh blackberries, sweetened

Assemble ingredients and utensils. In a medium bowl sift flour, sugar, salt, and baking powder together. Add milk and mix to a smooth batter. Spread batter in greased 9x9-inch pan or 1½-quart oven-proof glass dish. Pour butter evenly over the batter. Stir almond extract into the blackberries, and spoon blackberries over the batter. Bake in a preheated 350° oven for 45 minutes or until batter rises to top of dish and is brown. Yield: 6 to 8 servings.

HELPFUL HINT

When a recipe calls for "melted butter," (as opposed to "butter, melted") measure the product *after* it has been melted.

~

Peach-Pecan Cobbler

1   cup all-purpose flour
¼   cup quick-cooking rolled oats
¼   cup brown sugar, packed
1   teaspoon baking powder
½   teaspoon ground nutmeg
3   tablespoons butter or margarine
⅓   cup pecans, chopped
⅓   cup plus 1 tablespoon sugar
1   tablespoon cornstarch
¼   cup water
¼   teaspoon almond extract
4   cups peaches, sliced and peeled, or sliced
       nectarines, or frozen, unsweetened peach slices
1   egg
¼   cup whole milk
¼   teaspoon ground cinnamon
     peach ice cream, vanilla ice cream, or whipped
       cream (optional)

Assemble ingredients and utensils.

For biscuit topping, stir together flour, rolled oats, brown sugar, baking powder, and nutmeg in a medium bowl. Cut in butter or margarine with a pastry blender or two knives until mixture resembles coarse crumbs; add pecans. Make a well in the center of the dry mixture, then set dry mixture aside.

For filling, stir together the ⅓ cup sugar and cornstarch in a medium saucepan. Stir in water and almond extract; add fruit. Cook and stir over medium heat till slightly thickened and bubbly. Reduce heat and keep mixture hot.

Mix together egg and milk in a small bowl; add all at once to the dry biscuit topping and stir just till moistened. Transfer the hot filling to an ungreased 2-quart square glass baking dish. Immediately spoon biscuit topping into 8 mounds on top of the hot filling. Stir together the 1 tablespoon sugar and the cinnamon. Sprinkle over topping. Bake in a preheated 400° oven for 20 to 25 minutes or until a wooden toothpick inserted into the center of a dumpling comes out clean. Serve warm with peach or vanilla ice cream or whipped cream, if desired. Yield: 8 servings.

Fresh Pear Cobbler

8 ripe pears, peeled, cored, and cut into ¼-inch slices
1 tablespoon fresh ginger, grated
½ cup plus 3 tablespoons sugar
1½ tablespoons fresh lemon juice
  zest of 1 small lemon, finely grated
2 cups all-purpose flour
⅛ teaspoon salt
1½ teaspoons baking powder
2 tablespoons butter
⅓ cup solid vegetable shortening
1 egg
⅓ cup whole milk
  whipped cream and fresh ginger for garnish
  ice cream (optional)

Assemble ingredients and utensils. In a large bowl, combine pears, ginger, ½ cup sugar, lemon juice, and lemon zest; toss well and spoon into greased 2½ to 3-quart casserole baking dish. In a large bowl, combine flour, salt, baking powder, and 1 tablespoon sugar. Work the butter and shortening together with pastry blender or 2 knives until the mixture resemble coarse crumbs. In a separate bowl, lightly beat egg and milk together; slowly stir this into flour and shortening mixture. Knead lightly, sprinkling more and more flour if necessary to form a smooth and non-sticky dough. Break off portions of the dough and place them on top of the fruit, pressing lightly and flattening the dough. Cover the entire surface with the dough pieces to give a cobbled effect. Sprinkle remaining 2 tablespoons sugar over the dough. Bake in a preheated 425° oven 35 to 40 minutes, or until well browned. Serve with whipped cream and a pinch of ginger or with ice cream. Yield: 8 to 9 servings.

Miss Daisy

A cobbler is a homey food that everyone loves. It is a baked, deep-dish fruit dessert topped with a thick biscuit crust and sprinkled with spices and sugar. The biscuit dough should be rough and bumpy, like uneven cobblestones.

Quick Cobblers

½ cup butter
1 cup self-rising flour, sifted
1 cup sugar
¾ cup whole milk
1 can pie filling (apple, blueberry, or strawberry)
   whipped cream or ice cream (optional)

Assemble ingredients and utensils. Melt butter. Pour into casserole or square pan. Cover all sides of pan with the melted butter. In a medium bowl, combine flour and sugar, stir in the milk; batter will be the consistency of pancake batter. Pour batter into the pan on top of the melted butter; do not stir. Spoon your choice of pie filling over the batter. Bake in a preheated 350° oven for 45 to 50 minutes or until golden brown. Great topped with whipped cream or ice cream. Yield: 6 to 8 servings.

~

The following foods should not be frozen:

Gelatins
Refrigerator doughs
Potatoes and other
   water foods
Creamed cottage cheese
Sandwich spreads made
   with mayonnaise or
   boiled salad dressing
   and hard-cooked egg
   whites

Crisp salad-type
   materials such as
   tomatoes, greens,
   and cucumbers
Bananas and pears
Cakes with egg-based
   filling and/or icings
   containing egg whites
   or syrups
Cream or custard pies

A TIP FROM

Miss Daisy

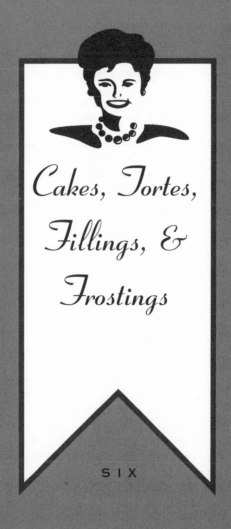

Cakes, Tortes,

Fillings, &

Frostings

SIX

Miss Daisy's Angel Food Cake

1½   cups egg whites (from about 8–10 large eggs)
1¼   teaspoons cream of tartar
¼   teaspoon salt
1   teaspoon vanilla
1½   cups sugar
1   cup all-purpose flour

Assemble all ingredients and utensils. In the large bowl of a mixer, beat egg whites, cream of tartar, salt, and vanilla until mixture holds a peak. Continue beating; add ½ cup sugar a little at a time. Sift together the flour and remaining sugar; then sift again over the egg whites. Fold in. Spoon batter into ungreased 10-inch tube pan. Bake in a preheated 375° oven for 30 minutes. When cake is done, immediately turn pan upside down to prevent cake from falling. Remove from pan when cool. Yield: 12 servings.

~

Icebox Pineapple Angel Food Cake

1   8-ounce can crushed pineapple with juice
     juice and grated zest of 1½ lemons
2   3-ounce packages lemon gelatin
3   cups heavy cream, whipped
1   Miss Daisy's Angel Food Cake (see recipe above)
     or 1 16-ounce prepared angel food cake
     mandarin oranges for garnish
     pineapple tidbits for garnish

Assemble ingredients and utensils. Using pineapple juice and lemon juice as the liquid, prepare gelatin. Chill until slightly thickened; mix in drained pineapple and grated zest. Fold in two-thirds of the whipped heavy cream. Break up angel food cake into small pieces and fold into pineapple mixture. Pour all into a lightly oiled tube pan. Chill for 24 hours. Garnish with remaining whipped cream, mandarin oranges, and pineapple pieces. Yield: 10 to 12 servings.

Lemon Coconut Angel Food Cake

1	Miss Daisy's Angel Food Cake (see facing page) or 1 16-ounce prepared angel food cake
2	tablespoons lemon zest, grated
½	cup lemon juice
3	eggs, beaten
¾	cup butter, softened
1	cup sugar
3	cups heavy cream, whipped
1½	cups grated fresh frozen coconut
3–4	tablespoons confectioners' sugar

HELPFUL HINT

This cake will keep in your refrigerator for two weeks.

Assemble ingredients and utensils. In the top of a double boiler, combine lemon zest, lemon juice, eggs, butter, and sugar; cook, stirring constantly, about 10 or 12 minutes until the mixture will coat a spoon. Let cool completely. Fold in one third of the whipped heavy cream and 1 cup coconut; chill. With a serrated or bakery knife, cut the cooled cake crosswise into 3 layers. Place the first layer on the cake plate and spread half the filling; top with the middle layer and spread with remaining filling. Place the last layer on top and frost entire cake with remaining whipped cream, sweetened with confectioners' sugar. Sprinkle remaining coconut all over. Refrigerate overnight or before serving. Yield: 12 large servings.

A TIP FROM

Miss Daisy

For a delicious variation of my Angel Food Cake recipe on the facing page, try Chocolate Angel Food Cake. Simply substitute ¼ cup cocoa for the ¼ cup of flour. This makes a great low-fat and low-cholesterol dessert!

Caramel Spice Cake

½ cup shortening
1⅓ cups sugar
2 large eggs
2 cups all-purpose flour
1 tablespoon baking powder
1 teaspoon salt
1 teaspoon ground cinnamon
½ teaspoon ground nutmeg
¼ teaspoon ground cloves
1 cup whole milk
1 teaspoon vanilla

Assemble ingredients and utensils. In the large bowl of a mixer, combine shortening, sugar, and eggs; mix until light and fluffy. In a separate bowl, sift dry ingredients. To the egg mixture, add dry ingredients alternately with milk; mix well after each addition; add vanilla. Pour into 2 greased and floured 8- or 9-inch layer pans. Bake in a preheated 350° oven for 35 to 40 minutes. Spread with caramel icing (see p. 138) or caramel frosting (see p. 112) Yield: 14 servings.

Gingerbread

1 cup light brown sugar
½ cup shortening
1 cup molasses
2 teaspoons baking powder
1 cup water, boiling
3 cups all-purpose flour
1 teaspoon ground ginger
1 teaspoon ground cinnamon
1 teaspoon ground allspice
1 teaspoon ground nutmeg
1 teaspoon ground cloves
½ teaspoon salt
2 eggs, well beaten

HELPFUL HINT

For a tasty variation, try topping Gingerbread with Lemon Sauce (see p. 138).

Assemble ingredients and utensils. In the large bowl of a mixer, combine all ingredients and mix well. Pour mixture into a greased bundt pan. Bake in a preheated 350° oven for 40 to 45 minutes or until done. Serve plain or with whipped cream or lemon sauce. Yield: 10 to 12 servings.

Fresh Carrot Cake with Cream Cheese Frosting

2   cups sifted all-purpose flour
2   teaspoons baking powder
1½   teaspoons baking soda
1½   teaspoons salt
2   teaspoons ground cinnamon
2   cups sugar
1½   cups vegetable oil
4   eggs
2   cups finely grated raw carrots, firmly packed
1   8½-ounce can crushed pineapple, drained
½   cup chopped walnuts, optional
1   3½-ounce can flaked coconut

Assemble ingredients and utensils. In the large bowl of a mixer, sift together flour, baking powder, baking soda, salt, and cinnamon. Gradually mix in sugar, oil, and eggs; beat well. Add carrots, pineapple, nuts, and coconut; blend thoroughly. Distribute batter evenly among 3 greased and floured 9-inch round cake pans. Bake in a preheated 350° oven for 35 to 40 minutes. Cool about 10 minutes in the pans. Turn out on wire racks and cool thoroughly. Fill layers and frost top and sides of cake with cream cheese frosting. Yield: 15 to 18 servings.

Cream Cheese Frosting

1   8-ounce package cream cheese, softened
½   cup butter, softened
1   16-ounce box confectioners' sugar
1   tablespoon vanilla
1   cup chopped walnuts or pecans, toasted

Assemble ingredients and utensils. In the large bowl of a mixer, combine cream cheese and butter. Mix until fluffy. Add sugar gradually; stir in vanilla; mix well. Stir in nuts. Yield 3½ cups.

~

My seven-year-old friend Jake McCoy loves to bake. Jake prepared this cake with me for Mother's Day on "Talk of the Town" on WTVF, the CBS affiliate in Nashville, Tennessee. Jake and the cake received rave reviews!

~

Fresh Blueberry Cheesecake

1	9-inch unbaked pie crust (see p. 74)
2	envelopes unflavored gelatin
1	cup half-and-half, cold
1	cup half-and-half, heated to boiling
6	ounces cream cheese, softened
½	cup sugar
2	tablespoons triple sec
1	teaspoon vanilla
1	cup ice cubes, about 6 to 8
2–2½	cups fresh blueberries
	whipped cream for garnish

Assemble ingredients and utensils. Press pastry into 10x2-inch
fluted quiche/flan pan or 9-inch deep-dish pie pan; prick
bottom and sides with fork. Bake in a preheated 450° oven for
10 minutes or until golden; cool. In a 5-cup blender or food
processor, sprinkle unflavored gelatin over cold half-and-half;
set aside 3 to 4 minutes. Add hot half-and-half and process at
low speed until gelatin is completely dissolved, about 2
minutes. Add cream cheese, sugar, triple sec, and vanilla;
process at high speed until blended. Add ice cubes, one at a
time; process at high speed until ice is melted. Set aside until
mixture is slightly thickened, about 5 minutes. Arrange 1 cup
blueberries in prepared crust; add gelatin mixture. Chill until
firm. Garnish with remaining blueberries and whipped cream.
Yield: About 8 servings.

Chocolate Cheesecake

Crust

25   chocolate wafers, crushed
6   tablespoons butter, melted
¼   teaspoon ground cinnamon

Assemble ingredients and utensils. Mix ingredients thoroughly and press into a well-buttered 10-inch springform pan. Chill crust.

Filling

3   8-ounce packages cream cheese, softened
1   cup sugar
3   eggs
8   ounces semi-sweet chocolate, melted and cooled
2   teaspoons cocoa
1   teaspoon vanilla
2   cups sour cream

Assemble ingredients and utensils. In the large bowl of a mixer, beat cream cheese until smooth and fluffy, add sugar, add eggs one at a time while beating. Stir in chocolate, cocoa, and vanilla; mix well. Add sour cream and beat until very smooth. Pour into crust. Bake in a preheated 350° oven for 1 hour and 10 minutes. Cool to room temperature and chill for at least 5 hours. Yield: 12-14 servings.

Peanutty Chocolate Cheesecakes

⅔ cup graham crackers, crushed
½ cup plus 2 tablespoons sugar
2 tablespoons butter, melted
1 8-ounce package plus 3 ounces cream cheese
1 teaspoon vanilla
½ cup whole milk
2 eggs
½ cup semi-sweet chocolate chips
¼ cup creamy peanut butter
   sweetened whipped cream or topping for garnish
   chopped peanuts for garnish

HELPFUL
HINT

Depending on
time needed
for cake
preparation,
turn on your
oven only 5
to 10 minutes
before
placing cake
in oven. This
keeps your
electricity bill
down and
keeps your
kitchen cool.

Assemble ingredients and utensils. Combine graham cracker crumbs, 2 tablespoons sugar, and butter in a small bowl. Press 1 level tablespoon of crumbs on bottom of 12 greased or paper-lined muffin tins (2½-inch diameter). In the small bowl of a mixer, combine 11 ounces of cream cheese, ½ cup sugar and vanilla. Beat until smooth and creamy. Add milk and eggs, beating just until blended. In the top of a double boiler, melt chocolate chips; gradually stir 1½ cups cheese mixture into melted chocolate. Add peanut butter to remaining cheese mixture, beating on low speed just until blended. Spoon 2 tablespoons of peanut butter mixture into each muffin cup. Spoon 2 tablespoons chocolate mixture evenly over the peanut butter mixture, filling cups almost full (mixture rises only slightly during baking). Bake in a preheated 325° oven for 20 to 25 minutes or until set. Cool on wire rack. Chill. To serve, peel off papers and garnish with sweetened whipped cream or topping and chopped peanuts. Yield: 12 servings.

Praline Cheesecake

1 cup graham crackers, crushed
3 tablespoons sugar
3 tablespoons butter, melted
3 8-ounce packages cream cheese, softened
1¼ cups dark brown sugar
2 tablespoons all-purpose flour
3 eggs
1½ teaspoons vanilla
1 cup pecans, finely chopped
maple syrup

Assemble ingredients and utensils. Combine graham cracker crumbs, sugar, and butter. Press into bottom of 9-inch springform pan. Bake at 350° for 10 minutes. In the large bowl of a mixer, blend cream cheese, brown sugar, and flour. Add eggs, one at a time, beating well after each addition. Add vanilla and ½ cup pecans; mix well. Pour into crumb crust. Bake in a preheated 350° oven for 50 to 55 minutes. Loosen from rim and cool. Remove sides of pan. Chill. Brush with maple syrup. Sprinkle with remaining pecans. Yield: 8 to 10 servings.

A TIP FROM

Miss Daisy

Slice cheesecakes and sticky iced cakes easily by dipping your knife into a tall glass of hot water before each slice.

Rum Cheesecake

2 cups graham crackers, crushed
½ cup butter, melted
4 8-ounce packages cream cheese, softened
⅛ teaspoon salt
2 teaspoons vanilla
4 eggs
1½ cup sugar
½ cup light rum
2 cups sour cream

Assemble ingredients and utensils. Combine graham cracker crumbs and butter; press into 9-inch pie plate. In the large bowl of a mixer, beat together cream cheese, salt, 1 teaspoon vanilla, eggs, 1 cup sugar, and rum until smooth. Pour into crust. Bake in a preheated 375° oven for 40 minutes. Cool 30 minutes. Combine sour cream, 1 teaspoon vanilla, and ½ cup sugar; pour over cake. Bake in a preheated 450° oven for 5 minutes. Refrigerate several days before serving to enhance the flavor. Yield: 6 to 8 servings.

Cheesecake with Strawberry Glaze

Crust

1	cup all-purpose flour, sifted
¼	cup sugar
1	teaspoon lemon zest, grated
½	teaspoon vanilla
1	egg yolk, beaten
½	cup butter, softened

Assemble ingredients and utensils. Mix the ingredients by hand in a small bowl and pat into the bottom of a 9-inch springform pan. Bake in a preheated 400° oven for 10 minutes. Cool.

Filling

2½	8-ounce packages cream cheese
¾	cup sugar
1¼	tablespoons all-purpose flour
¾	teaspoon vanilla
¾	teaspoon orange zest, grated
2	tablespoons sour cream
2	tablespoons whole milk or half-and-half
4	egg yolks

Assemble ingredients and utensils. In the medium bowl of a mixer, mix the cheese until softened. Beat in next 6 ingredients. Add egg yolks one at a time, beating well after each addition. Pour into springform pan over crust. Bake in a preheated 500° oven for about 6 minutes; then reduce temperature to 200° and cook for 30 minutes more. Do not overcook. Cool and refrigerate. Leave in springform pan until chilled, preferably overnight; then unmold and top with strawberry glaze.

Strawberry Glaze

2	pints fresh strawberries
¾	cup sugar
1½	tablespoons cornstarch
	juice of ½ lemon
3	drops red food coloring (optional)

Assemble ingredients and utensils. Pour 1 cup strawberries into blender and blend on high speed, making a purée. Place sugar and cornstarch in heavy saucepan; add strawberry purée slowly; add lemon juice and food coloring (if desired). Cook over medium heat until thick, stirring often, but do not overcook. Arrange remaining whole or halved strawberries on top of cheesecake and pour glaze over all. Decorate with more whole strawberries on top. Yield: 12 servings.

Fresh Coconut Cake

1   cup butter, softened
1   cup sugar
3½ cups all-purpose flour
3½ teaspoons baking powder
1   cup whole milk
½   teaspoon vanilla
½   teaspoon lemon flavoring
8   egg whites, stiffly beaten

Assemble ingredients and utensils. In the large bowl of a mixer, combine butter and sugar; add flour, baking powder, milk, vanilla, and lemon flavoring. Fold in stiffly beaten egg whites. Pour into 2 9-inch or 3 8-inch greased and floured cake pans. Bake in a preheated 350° oven for 30 to 35 minutes. Yield: 10 servings.

Icing

3   cups sugar
1   cup water
2   teaspoons apple cider vinegar
3   egg whites, beaten
½   teaspoon cream of tartar
1   teaspoon vanilla
1   teaspoon lemon flavoring
1½ cups fresh coconut, grated

Assemble ingredients and utensils. In a heavy saucepan, combine sugar, water, and vinegar; stir and cook until it reaches thread stage. In a separate bowl, beat egg whites and cream of tartar. Pour sugar mixture over egg whites; beat constantly. Add vanilla and lemon flavoring; stir in coconut. Spread on cool cake.

HELPFUL HINT

When making the icing for this cake, you will reach what is known as the thread stage, or 230°F to 234°F on a candy thermometer. The consistency will spin a thread when dropped from a spoon.

A TIP FROM
Miss Daisy

When buying fresh coconut, choose a coconut that's heavy, which means it's full of liquid. Shake it to check for the sound of the liquid. Coconut without liquid has spoiled. There are normally small rings on the end of the coconut.

Coconut Bavarian Custard Cake

1   Miss Daisy's Angel Food Cake (see p. 92), or
      1 16-ounce prepared cake, broken into
      bite-sized pieces
    sherry
1   cup sugar
2   tablespoons all-purpose flour
4   eggs, separated
1   teaspoon vanilla
2   cups whole milk
1   package unflavored gelatin dissolved in ¼ cup
      cold water
2   cups heavy cream, whipped
1   6-ounce package fresh frozen coconut, thawed

Assemble ingredients and utensils. Sprinkle cake pieces with sherry and set aside. In a small bowl, mix sugar, flour, and egg yolks, add vanilla and blend well. Stir milk into mixture and blend thoroughly. Cook in a heavy saucepan over low heat, stirring constantly until thickened (about 10 to 12 minutes). Stir in gelatin. Blend until gelatin is thoroughly dissolved; set mixture aside to cool. When cool, fold in half the whipped heavy cream and the stiffly beaten egg whites. In a large greased tube pan, alternate layers of broken cake pieces and sauce, ending with layer of sauce. Chill for at least 24 hours. When ready to serve, turn cake out onto serving platter. Frost with remaining whipped cream. Sprinkle generously with coconut. Yield: 12 to 14 servings.

German Chocolate Sour Cream Fudge Cake

1   18¼-ounce box German chocolate cake mix with
    pudding
3   eggs
1   cup milk
¾   cup vegetable oil

Assemble ingredients and utensils. Mix together and pour in
2 9-inch round cake pans. Bake in a preheated 350° oven for
30 minutes. Let cool.

Filling

2   cups sour cream
1½   cups sugar
3   cups sweetened flaked coconut
3   cups whipped topping or whipped cream, room
     temperature
1   teaspoon vanilla (optional)

Mix together, adding vanilla if desired. Split cake layers in
half. Put filling on top of each layer; stack and cover cake on
top and sides with filling. Keep in refrigerator.

Chocolate Buffet Cake

2   eggs, separated
1½   cup sugar
1¼   cups unsifted all-purpose flour
½   cup unsweetened cocoa
¾   teaspoon baking soda
½   teaspoon salt
½   cup vegetable oil
1   teaspoon vanilla
1   cup buttermilk or sour milk
      sweetened whipped cream
      raspberries for garnish

Assemble ingredients and utensils. Line a 15½x10½x1-inch
jelly roll pan with aluminum foil; generously grease and
flour foil. Set aside. Beat egg whites in the large bowl of a
mixer until foamy; gradually add ½ cup sugar, beating
until stiff peaks form. In another large bowl, combine
flour, 1 cup sugar, cocoa, soda, and salt. Add oil, vanilla,
buttermilk, and egg yolks; beat until smooth. Gently fold
egg whites into batter; spread evenly in prepared pan.
Bake in a preheated 350° oven for 25 to 30 minutes or
until cake springs back when lightly touched in center.
Cool 3 minutes; invert onto a large cooling rack.
Carefully remove foil; cool. Prepare chocolate rum filling.
Cut cake in half crosswise to form 2 equal pieces. Place
one layer on serving tray; spread with filling and top with
remaining layer. Chill while preparing glaze. Glaze cake;
refrigerate 2 to 3 hours or until set. To serve; top with
dollops or rosettes of sweetened whipped cream arranged
atop cake. Garnish with fresh raspberries, if desired.
Yield: 12 servings.

Chocolate Rum Filling

½   cup unsalted butter
⅔   cup sugar
⅓   cup unsweetened cocoa
1   egg
2   tablespoons dark rum
½   cup heavy cream, whipped

Assemble ingredients and utensils. In the small bowl of a
mixer, combine first 5 ingredients ; blend until smooth. Fold
in whipped heavy cream just until blended.

Chocolate Glaze

   2   tablespoons butter
   3   tablespoons unsweetened cocoa
   3   tablespoons water
   ½   teaspoon vanilla
   1¼ cups confectioners' sugar

Assemble ingredients and utensils. Melt butter in small saucepan over low heat. Stir in cocoa and water. Cook, stirring constantly until mixture thickens; do not boil. Remove from heat; stir in vanilla and confectioners' sugar, beating or whisking until smooth.

Three Chocolate Cake

   1   18¼-ounce package devil's food cake mix
        (or Devil's Food Cake p. 106)
   1   4⅛-ounce package instant chocolate pudding mix
   ½   cup brewed coffee
   4   large eggs
   1   cup sour cream
   ½   cup vegetable oil
   ½   cup Southern Comfort®
   2   cups semi-sweet chocolate chips

Assemble ingredients and utensils. In the large bowl of a mixer, combine all ingredients except chocolate chips. Blend on low speed. Beat at medium speed for one minute. Scrape bowl and beat one minute longer. Fold in chocolate chips. Pour into a greased and floured bundt pan. Bake in a preheated 350° oven for 55 to 60 minutes or until skewer inserted in center comes out clean. Turn out of pan and cool. Yield: 10 to 12 servings.

A NOTE FROM

Miss Daisy

Southern Comfort® was first created in 1874 by M. W. Heron, a young bartender in New Orleans. Heron developed a smooth amber spirit that has become known as "the Grand Old Drink of the South."

Is your cake done? For layer cakes and cupcakes, touch the cake lightly in the center with fingertip. It should spring back. The sides of the cake will also begin to pull away from the pan when it is done. For pound cakes, insert a skewer or toothpick in the center of the cake. It will come out clean when the cake is done.

A TIP FROM

Miss Daisy

Devil's Food Cake

4	1-ounce squares unsweetened chocolate
1¾	cups sugar
1	cup water
2¼	cups all-purpose flour, sifted
1½	teaspoons baking powder
1	teaspoon baking soda
½	teaspoon salt
¼	teaspoon ground cinnamon
1	cup butter
1	tablespoon vanilla
3	eggs
⅔	cup buttermilk

HELPFUL HINT

Orange Frosting (see p. 137) is delicious on this cake.

~

Assemble ingredients and utensils. In a heavy saucepan, combine chocolate, 1 cup sugar, and water; stir over low heat until thickened. Cool to room temperature, stirring occasionally. In a separate bowl, sift together flour, baking powder, soda, salt, and cinnamon. In the large bowl of a mixer, combine butter, add remaining ¾ cup sugar gradually and beat until smooth. Beat in vanilla and eggs one at a time, beating well after each addition. Beat in chocolate mixture. Add dry ingredients alternately with buttermilk, beginning and ending with dry ingredients, stirring until batter is smooth. Pour into 2 greased and floured 9-inch round layer pans. Bake in a preheated 350° oven for 30 minutes until cake is done. Cool in pans for 10 minutes. Fill and frost top and sides of cake as desired. Yield: 12 to 14 servings.

Fudge Cake

1 cup butter
4 ounces bitter chocolate
4 eggs
2 cups sugar
1 cup all-purpose flour
1 teaspoon vanilla
1 cup nuts, chopped
  ice cream or whipped cream (optional)

Assemble ingredients and utensils. In a heavy saucepan, melt butter and chocolate over low heat. In the large bowl of a mixer, combine eggs, sugar, and flour. Add chocolate mixture, vanilla, and nuts to flour mixture and stir. Pour in 2 8-inch square pans which have been greased and floured. Bake in a preheated 275° oven for 45 to 50 minutes. Top with icing, ice cream, or whipped cream. Yield: 18 servings (9 per pan).

Icing

½ cup butter
2 1-ounce squares unsweetened baking chocolate
1 16-ounce box confectioners' sugar
5 tablespoons evaporated milk
1 teaspoon vanilla

Assemble ingredients and utensils. In a heavy saucepan, melt butter and chocolate. Add sugar, milk, and vanilla. Mix until creamy.

HELPFUL HINT

Let a cake cool completely before slicing or icing.

Sour Cream Chocolate Cake

2 cups all-purpose flour
2 cups sugar
1 cup water
¾ cup sour cream
¼ cup butter
1¼ teaspoons baking soda
1 teaspoon salt
1 teaspoon vanilla
½ teaspoon baking powder
2 eggs
4 1-ounce squares unsweetened baking chocolate, melted

Assemble ingredients and utensils. Measure all of the ingredients for the cake into the large bowl of mixer and beat for 30 seconds at low speed, scraping the sides of the bowl constantly; then beat for 3 minutes at high speed. Pour into greased and floured cake pans, either 2 9-inch pans or 3 8-inch pans. Bake in a preheated 350° oven for 20 to 25 minutes. Remove from the oven and cool on racks. Frost. Yield: 8 to 10 servings.

Frosting

½ cup butter
4 1-ounce squares unsweetened baking chocolate
4 cups confectioners' sugar
1 cup sour cream
2 teaspoons vanilla

Assemble ingredients and utensils. In the top of a double boiler, melt butter and chocolate over barely simmering water. Remove from heat and cool. Add confectioners' sugar, blend in sour cream and vanilla, and beat until smooth. Put frosting between each of the layers of the cake, on the top, and all around the sides.

HELPFUL HINT

For even slices, cut a whole cake in half, then in quarters, and then into the desired number of pieces.

Pecan Fruit Cake

8 ounces candied cherries (red or green)
8 ounce box pitted dates (may be pre-chopped)
6 slices candied pineapple
1 pound (4 cups) pecans, halved
1 cup self-rising flour
4 eggs
1 teaspoon vanilla
1 tablespoon Southern Comfort®

Assemble ingredients and utensils. Chop cherries in half. Chop dates and pineapple coarsely. Coarsely chop pecans into fairly large pieces. Sift flour over fruit and nuts to coat well. Beat eggs until yolks and whites are well blended, then add sugar, vanilla, and Southern Comfort®. Beat until dissolved. Add to fruit-nut mixture and mix thoroughly (until all flour is moistened). Line tube pan with waxed paper, then grease. Pour batter into tube pan and bake in a preheated 350° oven for 1 hour and 45 minutes with a pan of water on lower shelf during the last 15 minutes of baking time. Turn out of pan onto rack to cool completely. Slice thin to serve. Yield: 10 to 12 servings

A TIP FROM

Miss Daisy

Fruitcake lasts a long time if it is kept in cake tins wrapped in cheesecloth that has been soaked in Southern Comfort®. Keep the cheesecloth damp with Southern Comfort® throughout the life of the fruit-cake. Remember that fruitcakes and pound cakes are easier to slice when they are cold.

Oatmeal Cake

**HELPFUL
HINT**

Oatmeal Cake
is great for
morning
coffee or
brunches.

2	cups quick-cooking rolled oats
3	cups boiling water
4	eggs
2	cups sugar
2	cups brown sugar
1	cup shortening
3	cups all-purpose flour
2	teaspoons ground cinnamon
2	teaspoons baking soda
1	teaspoon salt

Assemble ingredients and utensils. Cook oats in water; set aside. In the large bowl of a mixer, combine together eggs, sugars, and shortening, add remaining ingredients and beat well; stir in oatmeal. Bake in 2 13x9-inch greased pans in a preheated 350° oven for 30 to 35 minutes or until a skewer inserted in center comes out clean. Prepare topping and pour over cake. Yield: 10 to 12 servings.

Topping

1	cup pecans, chopped
1	pound brown sugar
1	cup butter
1	cup whole milk
2	cups fresh frozen coconut
1	teaspoon vanilla

Assemble ingredients and utensils. In a heavy saucepan, mix together and bring to a rapid boil in a saucepan. Pour over hot cake.

Italian Cream Cake

½ cup butter
½ cup vegetable oil
2 cups sugar
5 eggs, separated
1 cup buttermilk
1 teaspoon baking soda
2 cups all-purpose flour, sifted
1 teaspoon vanilla
1 cup sweetened flaked coconut
½ cup nuts, chopped (walnuts or pecans)

Assemble ingredients and utensils. In the large bowl of a mixer, combine butter, oil, and sugar; blend well. Add egg yolks one at a time, beating after each addition. In a small bowl, stir baking soda into buttermilk. Add small amount of flour to egg yolk mixture, beating at medium speed, alternating with buttermilk mixture. Add vanilla, coconut, and pecans. In a separate bowl, beat egg whites until stiff and fold into cake batter. Pour into a greased and floured 9x13-inch cake pan or 3 greased and floured 8-inch layer pans. Bake in a preheated 325° oven for 45 minutes. Cool and spread with icing. Yield: 15 to 18 servings.

Icing

1 8-ounce package cream cheese, softened
½ cup butter, softened
1 16-ounce box confectioners' sugar
1 teaspoon vanilla
½ cup nuts, chopped (walnuts or pecans)

Assemble ingredients and utensils. In the large bowl of a mixer, beat cream cheese and butter. Add sugar and vanilla; mix well. Add nuts; mix. Spread on cake.

A TIP FROM

Miss Daisy

Italian Cream Cake is always a blue ribbon recipe, and it will bring you many compliments! It also makes a wonderful wedding cake.

~

Strawberry Jam Cake

HELPFUL HINT

When icing a cake, dust a little cornstarch or flour on before icing. This will prevent the icing from sliding off.

2	cups all-purpose flour, sifted
1	cup light brown sugar
1	teaspoon ground cinnamon
½	teaspoon ground cloves
¼	teaspoon salt
1	cup butter, softened
3	eggs, beaten
1	teaspoon baking soda
½	cup buttermilk
1½	cups strawberry jam
½	cup pecans, chopped

Assemble ingredients and utensils. Sift dry ingredients in a large bowl. Gradually blend in butter and add eggs. Mix well. Dissolve baking soda in buttermilk and mix into creamed mixture. Continue beating for 3 minutes. Add jam and pecans, mix well. Grease and flour a 9x13-inch pan. Pour batter into pan and bake in a preheated 350° oven for 55-60 minutes. Cool. Ice with caramel frosting. Yield: 24 servings.

Caramel Frosting

½	cup butter
¼	cup whole milk
1	cup light brown sugar
2	cups confectioners' sugar, sifted

Assemble ingredients and utensils. In a large saucepan, melt butter and brown, but do not burn. Bring to a full boil for 2 minutes stirring constantly. Add milk, bring to a full boil again. Cool just to lukewarm, and then add sugars, mix well, and pour over cool cake. Yield: about 2 cups.

You can grease and line the bottom of cake pans with waxed paper, butter, non-stick spray, or oil.

A TIP FROM

Miss Daisy

Blackberry Jam Cake

1   cup butter, softened
2   cups sugar
6   eggs
3   cups all-purpose flour
1   teaspoon ground nutmeg
1   teaspoon ground cinnamon
1   teaspoon ground cloves
6   tablespoons buttermilk
2   teaspoons baking soda
2   cups blackberry jam
2   teaspoons vanilla

Assemble ingredients and utensils. In the large bowl of a mixer, combine softened butter and sugar; add eggs one at a time, beating well after each addition until fluffy. In a separate mixing bowl, combine flour with spices. In another bowl, combine buttermilk and soda. Add dry flour and spice mixture alternately with buttermilk mixture to creamed butter, sugar, and egg mixture until blended well. Add jam and vanilla; mix well. Pour into 4 greased and floured 8-inch cake pans. Bake in a preheated 350° oven for 20 to 25 minutes until cake tests done. Yield: 16 servings.

Filling

4   eggs
3   cups sugar
2   cups raisins
2   cups whole milk
2   tablespoons all-purpose flour
2   cups sweetened flaked coconut

Assemble ingredients and utensils. In a heavy saucepan, combine all ingredients. Cook until thick and spread between layers and on the top and sides of the jam cake.

A TIP FROM

Miss Daisy

When pouring cake batter into the pan, level the batter by tapping the pan on the top of the counter. This will prevent air holes from forming.

Orange Slice Cake

3½ cups all-purpose flour
1½ teaspoons salt
1   18-ounce bag candy orange slices
1   8-ounce box pitted dates, chopped
2   cups pecans, chopped
1   3½-ounce can sweetened flaked coconut
1   cup butter, softened
2   cups sugar
4   eggs
½   cup buttermilk
1½ teaspoons baking soda
1   tablespoon vanilla

Assemble ingredients and utensils. In a medium bowl, sift together flour and salt; set aside. In a separate bowl, add ½ cup of flour mixture to the next 4 ingredients. In the large bowl of a mixer, beat butter and sugar well; add eggs one at a time, mixing well after each addition. In a separate bowl, add baking soda to buttermilk. Add flour mixture alternately with buttermilk mixture to the butter and sugar mixture. Add the orange mixture; add vanilla. Pour into greased and floured 10-inch tube pan. Bake in a preheated 300° oven for 1 hour and 45 minutes until top is crusty. Drizzle top immediately with glaze. Cool. Let cake stand in refrigerator overnight before removing from pan. Yield: 14 large servings.

Glaze
1   cup orange juice
2   cups confectioners' sugar

Assemble ingredients and utensils. In a medium bowl, mix ingredients; stir until syrupy. Pour over hot cake.

To remove cake layers, cool the cakes on a wire rack away from drafts for about 10 minutes. Loosen the edges with a metal spatula. Invert the cake pan on the rack. Tap the bottom of the pan and then remove it. Sheet cakes can be cooled in the pan.

A TIP FROM

Miss Daisy

Elegant Orange Cake

1   cup butter, softened
2   cups sugar
4   eggs, separated
2   teaspoons vanilla
2⅔ cups all-purpose flour
2½ teaspoons baking powder
½   teaspoon salt
1   cup whole milk
2   tablespoons orange zest, grated

Assemble ingredients and utensils. In the large bowl of a mixer, blend together butter and sugar until smooth. Beat in egg yolks one at a time, mixing thoroughly. Stir in vanilla. Sift flour, baking powder, and salt; add to butter mixture, alternating with milk. Beat egg whites until stiff and fold into batter. Pour into 3 greased and floured 9-inch cake pans. Bake in a preheated 350° oven for 35 to 40 minutes, or until toothpick inserted in the center comes out clean. Remove from oven when done and cool on racks. Yield: 12 to 14 servings.

Filling

1   cup sugar
1   teaspoon orange zest, grated
6   tablespoons all-purpose flour
¼   cup fresh orange juice
2   eggs, beaten
2   cups heavy cream, whipped

Assemble ingredients and utensils. In the top of a double boiler, combine sugar, orange zest, and flour; stir in orange juice and eggs. Cook, stirring constantly, over simmering water until thickened. Cool and fold into whipped heavy cream. Spread between the layers of the cake.

Frosting

6   ounces cream cheese, softened
1   tablespoon fresh orange juice
2½ cups confectioners' sugar
2   teaspoons orange zest, grated
    fresh mint for garnish

Assemble ingredients and utensils. In a bowl, combine all ingredients thoroughly. Frost top and sides of cake. Decorate top of the cake with grated orange zest, or sections of mandarin oranges, placing a sprig of mint in the center of the cake.

Miss Daisy's Strawberry Cake

1   18¼-ounce package yellow or white cake mix
1   3-ounce package strawberry gelatin
¾   cup vegetable oil
1   cup pecans, chopped
4   eggs
2   tablespoons all-purpose flour
1   10-ounce package frozen sliced sweetened
      strawberries, thawed or 1 pint fresh strawberries,
      sliced and mixed with ½ cup sugar
      whipped cream for garnish

Assemble ingredients and utensils. In the large bowl of a
mixer, combine cake mix, strawberry gelatin, vegetable oil,
nuts, eggs, flour, and strawberries. Beat at medium speed
for 3 minutes or until blended. Pour batter into a greased
and floured 10-inch tube or bundt pan. Bake in a preheated
350° oven for 55 to 60 minutes or until inserted toothpick
comes out clean. While cake is warm, pour glaze over top,
or serve plain with sweetened whipped cream. Yield: 12 to
14 servings.

Glaze
1   cup sugar
½   cup water
2   tablespoons butter
1   teaspoon vanilla or banana flavoring

Assemble ingredients and utensils. In a heavy saucepan, bring
sugar, water, and butter to a boil; add vanilla or banana
flavoring. Punch holes in the top of the cake; drizzle over the
top and sides while hot so the glaze penetrates the cake.

Pecan Bourbon Cake

½ pound seedless raisins, cut in half
2 teaspoons ground nutmeg
⅔ cup plus 2–3 tablespoons bourbon
3 cups all-purpose flour
1½ teaspoons baking powder
1 teaspoon salt
½ cup butter
½ cup shortening
1½ cups sugar
1 teaspoon vanilla
6 eggs
2 cups pecans, chopped
confectioners' sugar for garnish

Assemble ingredients and utensils. In a small bowl, combine raisins, nutmeg, and ⅔ cup bourbon; let stand for about 30 minutes. In a separate bowl, sift together flour, baking powder, and salt. In the large bowl of a mixer, combine butter and shortening until fluffy; add sugar gradually and mix until light. Add vanilla. Beat in eggs one at a time, beating well after each addition. Add dry ingredients alternately with raisin/bourbon mixture, beginning and ending with dry ingredients. Stir until all dry ingredients are moistened. Pour into greased and floured 10-inch tube pan. Bake in a preheated 325° oven for 1 hour and 15 minutes, until cake tester inserted in the center of the cake comes out clean. Cool in pan for 15 minutes; turn cake out of pan and finish cooling on wire rack. If desired, drizzle 2 or 3 tablespoons of bourbon over cake. Wrap in foil. Store for 2 to 3 days in refrigerator before serving. Just before serving, sift confectioners' sugar over the top. Yield: 12 to 14 servings.

A TIP FROM
Miss Daisy

You may bake cakes as layers, loaves, sheets, tubes, or cupcakes—but many recipes can't be used interchangeably. To be safe, use the type and size pan specified in the recipe. Place pans as near the center of the oven as possible. Don't let pans touch each other or sides of oven. Don't place pans directly under each other. If necessary, stagger the pans on two shelves.

If you are entertaining a large group of guests, at a wedding or a family reunion for example, you will need 8 two-layer cakes (a two-layer cake is the same as 1 whole bundt cake), or 2 18x25-inch sheet cakes to feed one hundred people.

A TIP FROM

Miss Daisy

Pumpkin Cake

HELPFUL HINT

This recipe can also be used to make cupcakes, which are fun at Halloween and Thanksgiving.

~

4	eggs
2	cups sugar
1	cup vegetable oil
2	cups all-purpose flour
1/8	teaspoon salt
2	teaspoons baking soda
2	teaspoons ground cinnamon
2	cups pumpkin pie filling

Assemble ingredients and utensils. In the large bowl of a mixer, combine together eggs, sugar, and oil. Add sifted dry ingredients. Blend in pumpkin pie filling. Pour into greased 12x18-inch pan. Bake in a preheated 350° oven for 25 to 30 minutes. Frost with cream cheese frosting. Cut into squares to serve. Yield: 12 to 15 servings.

Cream Cheese Frosting

1/2	cup butter, softened
1	16-ounce box confectioners' sugar
1	8-ounce package cream cheese, softened
1	teaspoon vanilla
1	cup walnuts, chopped

Assemble ingredients and utensils. Mix and spread over cooled pumpkin cake.

Red Velvet Cake

A NOTE FROM

Miss
Daisy

Most culinary
historians in
the South
attribute the
popularity of
Red Velvet
Cake to the
Regas family,
whose
Knoxville,
Tennessee,
restaurants
are legendary.
Grady Regas,
who can
usually be
found at
Regas
Riverside
Tavern or
Regas Cafe,
has many
stories to tell
about Red
Velvet Cake.
If you can't
make it to
Regas, be sure
to try this
delicious
recipe!

½ cup butter
½ cup shortening
2 cups sugar
4 eggs
2½ cups all-purpose flour
1 teaspoon baking soda
¼ teaspoon salt
4 tablespoons cocoa
1 cup buttermilk
1 teaspoon vanilla
4 tablespoons red food coloring

Assemble ingredients and utensils. In a bowl of large mixer, combine the butter, shortening, and sugar until creamy. Add eggs one at a time. Combine flour, baking soda, salt, and cocoa, and gradually add to butter mixture alternating with buttermilk. Add vanilla and food coloring. Blend well. Pour into 3 greased and floured 9-inch cake pans or 1 tube pan. Bake in a preheated 350° oven for 25 to 30 minutes or until a skewer inserted in center comes out clean. Cool cake. Prepare frosting and ice cake. Yield: 10 to 12 servings.

Frosting

1 16-ounce box confectioners' sugar
1 cup butter, softened
1 teaspoon vanilla
4 tablespoons heavy cream
½ cup sweetened flaked coconut
 red food coloring

Assemble ingredients and utensils. Blend confectioners' sugar, butter, vanilla, and heavy cream with mixer until smooth and fluffy. Additional cream may be needed to achieve fluffy consistency. Frost layers and assemble. Tint coconut with red food coloring and sprinkle over top.

~

Raspberry Blackberry Cake

1   18¼-ounce package white cake mix
1   3-ounce package blackberry gelatin
⅔   cup blackberry juice
⅔   cup vegetable oil
4   eggs

Assemble ingredients and utensils. In the large bowl of a mixer, combine cake mix, gelatin, blackberry juice, oil, and eggs; mix well. Pour into greased and floured 9x13-inch pan. Bake in a preheated 325° oven for 40 to 45 minutes. Spread with topping. Yield: 12 to 16 servings.

Topping

1   15-ounce can blackberries, drained
2   tablespoons brown sugar
1   3-ounce package raspberry gelatin
1   teaspoon cornstarch

Assemble ingredients and utensils. In a heavy saucepan, combine all ingredients and cook until thickened. Chill in refrigerator. Pour on top of cooled cake.

Miss Daisy's Pineapple Upside-Down Cake

¼   cup butter
1   cup dark brown sugar, firmly packed
7   canned Dole® pineapple slices, drained (reserve liquid)
1   18¼-ounce package white cake mix
2   egg whites
1   cup sugar
⅓   cup pineapple juice (drained from slices)

Assemble ingredients and utensils. In an iron skillet (preferably size #8), melt butter and sprinkle brown sugar evenly over the melted butter; arrange pineapple over the brown sugar. In the large bowl of a mixer, combine remaining ingredients; beat 2 minutes at medium speed. Pour cake batter into skillet. Bake in a preheated 350° oven for 35 to 40 minutes. Invert. Serve warm. Yield: 6 to 8 servings.

Pumpkin Cake

4	eggs
2	cups sugar
1	cup vegetable oil
2	cups all-purpose flour
⅛	teaspoon salt
2	teaspoons baking soda
2	teaspoons ground cinnamon
2	cups pumpkin pie filling

Assemble ingredients and utensils. In the large bowl of a mixer, combine together eggs, sugar, and oil. Add sifted dry ingredients. Blend in pumpkin pie filling. Pour into greased 12x18-inch pan. Bake in a preheated 350° oven for 25 to 30 minutes. Frost with cream cheese frosting. Cut into squares to serve. Yield: 12 to 15 servings.

Cream Cheese Frosting

½	cup butter, softened
1	16-ounce box confectioners' sugar
1	8-ounce package cream cheese, softened
1	teaspoon vanilla
1	cup walnuts, chopped

Assemble ingredients and utensils. Mix and spread over cooled pumpkin cake.

Pecan Bourbon Cake

½ pound seedless raisins, cut in half
2 teaspoons ground nutmeg
⅔ cup plus 2–3 tablespoons bourbon
3 cups all-purpose flour
1½ teaspoons baking powder
1 teaspoon salt
½ cup butter
½ cup shortening
1½ cups sugar
1 teaspoon vanilla
6 eggs
2 cups pecans, chopped
   confectioners' sugar for garnish

Assemble ingredients and utensils. In a small bowl, combine raisins, nutmeg, and ⅔ cup bourbon; let stand for about 30 minutes. In a separate bowl, sift together flour, baking powder, and salt. In the large bowl of a mixer, combine butter and shortening until fluffy; add sugar gradually and mix until light. Add vanilla. Beat in eggs one at a time, beating well after each addition. Add dry ingredients alternately with raisin/bourbon mixture, beginning and ending with dry ingredients. Stir until all dry ingredients are moistened. Pour into greased and floured 10-inch tube pan. Bake in a preheated 325° oven for 1 hour and 15 minutes, until cake tester inserted in the center of the cake comes out clean. Cool in pan for 15 minutes; turn cake out of pan and finish cooling on wire rack. If desired, drizzle 2 or 3 tablespoons of bourbon over cake. Wrap in foil. Store for 2 to 3 days in refrigerator before serving. Just before serving, sift confectioners' sugar over the top. Yield: 12 to 14 servings.

A TIP FROM
Miss Daisy

You may bake cakes as layers, loaves, sheets, tubes, or cupcakes—but many recipes can't be used interchangeably. To be safe, use the type and size pan specified in the recipe. Place pans as near the center of the oven as possible. Don't let pans touch each other or sides of oven. Don't place pans directly under each other. If necessary, stagger the pans on two shelves.

Miss Daisy's Five Flavor Pound Cake with Glaze

1   cup butter, softened
½   cup vegetable shortening
3   cups sugar
6   eggs, well beaten
3   cups all-purpose flour, sifted
½   teaspoon baking powder
1   cup whole milk
1   teaspoon *each*: coconut, butter, lemon, rum, and
      vanilla extracts

Assemble ingredients and utensils. In the large bowl of a mixer, combine butter, shortening, and sugar until light and fluffy. Add eggs. Combine flour and baking powder. Add to cream mixture alternately with milk. Stir in extracts. Spoon batter into a greased 10-inch tube pan. Bake in a preheated 325° oven for 1½ hours or until cake tests done. Add glaze and cool in pan about 10 minutes before turning out. Yield: 14 to 16 slices.

Glaze

1   cup sugar
½   cup water
1   teaspoon *each*: coconut, butter, lemon, rum, and
      vanilla extracts

Assemble ingredients and utensils. In a saucepan, combine all ingredients and gently bring to a boil. Pour over cake in pan. Let cake sit in pan until cool.

A NOTE FROM

Miss Daisy

My grandmother Linnie Angeline Fraser Deaton of Hall County, Georgia, was the proud recipient of a blue ribbon for a version of this cake in 1904. Later that year, she served the cake to my grandfather, which won his heart, and then she became his bride.

A TIP FROM

Miss Daisy

For an added treat, frost with Chocolate Satin Frosting (see p. 138).

Miss Daisy's Sour Cream Vanilla Pound Cake

½ cup butter, softened
½ cup shortening
3 cups sugar
6 egg yolks
1 teaspoon salt
3 cups all-purpose flour, sifted
¼ teaspoon baking soda
1 8-ounce carton sour cream
1 tablespoon vanilla

Assemble ingredients and utensils. In the large bowl of a mixer, combine butter and shortening; add sugar and beat well. Add egg yolks, beating well after each addition. In a separate bowl, sift dry ingredients together. Add dry ingredients alternately with sour cream to the egg/butter mixture; add vanilla. Pour into greased and floured 10-inch tube or bundt pan. Bake in a preheated 300° oven for 1½ hours. Yield: 12 to 14 servings.

Miss Daisy's Lemon Poppy Seed Cake

1 18¼-ounce package yellow cake mix
1 6-ounce package lemon instant pudding mix
½ cup vegetable oil
1 cup water
4 eggs
¼ cup poppy seeds

Assemble ingredients and utensils. In the large bowl of a mixer, combine all ingredients. Pour into a greased and floured bundt or 10-inch tube pan. Bake in a preheated 350° oven for 1 hour. Drizzle with glaze. Yield: 12 to 14 servings.

Glaze
1 cup sugar
½ cup water
1 teaspoon lemon extract

Assemble ingredients and utensils. In a heavy saucepan, bring sugar and water to a boil; add extract; boil for 3 minutes. Drizzle glaze over cake while hot.

Miss Daisy's Black Walnut Coconut Pound Cake

2	cups sugar
1	cup oil
4	eggs, beaten
3	cups all-purpose flour
½	teaspoon baking powder
1	cup buttermilk
1	cup black walnuts, chopped
1	cup sweetened flaked coconut
2	teaspoons coconut extract

HELPFUL HINT

Pound cakes freeze well. The freezer creates extra moisture for the cakes.

Assemble ingredients and utensils. In the large bowl of a mixer, combine sugar, oil, and eggs; beat well. Combine all dry ingredients. Add to sugar and egg mixture, alternately with buttermilk. Stir in walnuts, coconut, and extract. Pour batter into well-greased and floured 10-inch tube pan or bundt cake pan. Bake in a preheated 325° oven for one hour or until done. Pour hot coconut syrup over hot cake. Let cake remain in pan for several hours to absorb all the syrup. Cake will be very moist. Yield: 12 to 14 servings.

Coconut Syrup

1	cup sugar
½	cup water
3	tablespoons butter
1½	teaspoons coconut extract

Assemble ingredients and utensils. In a saucepan, combine sugar, water, and butter. Bring to a boil; boil 5 minutes. Remove from heat and stir in extract. Pour hot syrup over cake.

Miss Daisy's Pineapple Pound Cake

1	cup butter, softened
½	cup shortening
2¾	cups sugar
6	eggs
3	cups all-purpose flour
1½	teaspoons baking powder
¼	cup whole milk
1	teaspoon vanilla
¾	cup Dole® crushed pineapple, undrained

Assemble ingredients and utensils. In the large bowl of a mixer, combine butter, shortening, and sugar; mix until light and fluffy. Add eggs one at a time, beating after each addition. In a separate bowl, combine flour and baking powder; add to creamed mixture alternately with milk. Add vanilla, beating well. Stir in crushed pineapple. Pour batter into a well-greased and floured 10-inch tube or bundt pan. Place in cold oven. Then set temperature at 325° and bake for for 1 hour and 15 minutes or until cake tests done. Invert and cool. Drizzle pineapple glaze. Yield: 12 to 14 servings.

Pineapple Glaze

1½	cups confectioners' sugar
¼	cup butter, melted
1	cup Dole® crushed pineapple, drained.

Assemble ingredients and utensils. In large mixing bowl, combine sugar and butter, mix until smooth. Stir in pineapple. Punch holes in the top of the cake; drizzle over top so the glaze penetrates the cake.

~

Miss Daisy's Butter-Rum Cake

1   cup pecans, chopped
1   18¼-ounce package yellow cake mix
1   3¾-ounce package vanilla instant pudding
4   eggs
½   cup water, cold
½   cup vegetable oil
½   cup dark rum
½   cup butterscotch morsels

Assemble ingredients and utensils. Grease and flour 10-inch tube or bundt pan. Sprinkle nuts over bottom of pan. In the large bowl of a mixer, combine remaining ingredients. Pour batter over nuts in pan. Bake in a preheated 325° oven for 1 hour. Set on rack to cool. Invert on cake plate. Drizzle top and sides with glaze. Sprinkle with butterscotch morsels. Yield: 12 to 14 servings.

Glaze

½   cup butter
1   cup sugar
½   cup water
½   cup dark rum

Assemble ingredients and utensils. In a heavy saucepan, melt butter and sugar; stir in water. Boil 5 minutes, stirring constantly; remove from heat. Stir in rum. Drizzle over cake.

A TIP FROM

Miss Daisy

Most cake recipes call for all-purpose flour. You can substitute cake flour to produce a more velvety product. If you use cake flour, reduce the all-purpose flour amount called for in the recipe by 2 tablespoons per cup.

Miss Daisy's Chocolate Coffee Pound Cake

3	cups all-purpose flour, sifted
1½	teaspoons baking powder
½	teaspoon salt
4	1-ounce squares unsweetened chocolate
¼	cup strong brewed coffee
1	cup butter, softened
3	cups sugar
5	eggs
⅔	cup heavy cream
2	teaspoons vanilla extract
2	tablespoons Jack Daniel's® Tennessee Whiskey
	whipped cream (optional)

Assemble ingredients and utensils. In a bowl, combine flour, baking powder, and salt. Sift again and set aside. In the top of a double boiler, heat the chocolate and coffee. Stir constantly until smooth and satiny. Set aside to cool. In the large bowl of a mixer, combine the butter and sugar. Add eggs and beat hard until the mixture is smooth. Add the flour alternately with the chocolate/coffee mixture and heavy cream. Blend in the vanilla and Jack Daniel's®. Spoon batter into a well-greased and floured 10-inch tube or bundt pan and bake in a preheated 300° oven for 1½ to 1¾ hours. Cool before slicing. Serve with whipped cream or your favorite sauce. Yield: 12 servings.

When slicing a cake, dip your knife into hot water before each slice. Always hold the knife at a pitched position. Don't come straight down—it will mash the cake. When cutting a round cake, start at the center and work towards the edges: place the knife point at the center, go down with the point, and then gradually bring down the rest of the blade.

A TIP FROM

Miss Daisy

Chocolate Chip Cupcakes

1½ cups cake flour
1   cup sugar
1   teaspoon baking soda
½   teaspoon salt
¼   cup unsweetened cocoa
½   cup vegetable oil
1   cup water
1   teaspoon vanilla
1   tablespoon white distilled vinegar
    paper muffin baking cups

Assemble ingredients and utensils. In the medium bowl of a mixer, sift together cake flour, sugar, baking soda, salt, and cocoa. Add oil, water, vanilla, and vinegar, mix well. Fill greased or paper-lined muffin tins a third full with cake batter and with a rounded tablespoon of the topping. Bake in a preheated 350° oven for 18 to 20 minutes. Yield: 12 cupcakes.

Topping

1   8-ounce package cream cheese
1   egg
⅓   cup sugar
⅛   teaspoon salt
6   ounces of semi-sweet chocolate chips

Assemble ingredients and utensils. In a small bowl, combine first four ingredients; stir in chocolate chips.

Fudge Brownie Cupcakes

4   1-ounce squares semi-sweet chocolate
1   cup butter
1   cup pecans, chopped
1¾ cups sugar
1   cup all-purpose flour
4   eggs
1   teaspoon vanilla

Assemble ingredients and utensils. In a saucepan, melt chocolate and butter together; add nuts and stir until well coated. In a mixing bowl, combine sugar, flour, and unbeaten eggs; mix until well blended but do not beat. Stir in vanilla. Add chocolate mixture. Completely fill greased or paper-lined muffin tins. Bake in a preheated 350° oven for 40 to 50 minutes. Yield: 12 cupcakes.

A NOTE FROM

Miss Daisy

Both of these cupcake recipes are favorites of my young friend Caroline Gettelfinger.

HELPFUL HINT
FROM
Caroline

For a birthday party, let your friends ice their own cupcakes and add sprinkles, cookie crumbles, and candy.

Chocolate Nut Torte

¾   cup butter
¾   cup sugar
7   eggs, separated
4   1-ounce squares sweetened baking chocolate,
     melted and cooled
1   cup unblanched almonds, finely ground
½   teaspoon baking powder
¼   cup unblanched almonds, chopped

Assemble ingredients and utensils. In the large bowl of a mixer, add butter, gradually beat in sugar until the mixture is light and creamy. Beat in egg yolks one at a time. Blend in chocolate. Gently fold in ground almonds that have been mixed with baking powder. Beat egg whites until stiff, but not dry, then fold into chocolate mixture. Pour into 2 well-greased 9-inch layer cake pans. Bake in a preheated 350 oven for about 30 minutes. Cool. Frost between the layers and over the top of the torte with filling. Sprinkle with chopped nuts. Yield: 12 servings.

Chocolate Filling

4   eggs, lightly beaten
¼   cup sugar
½   teaspoon cornstarch
4   1-ounce squares sweetened baking chocolate,
     melted
½   cup butter, softened
½   cup walnuts, finely ground
1   teaspoon vanilla

Assemble ingredients and utensils. In the top of a double boiler, mix together eggs, sugar, and cornstarch. Heat over boiling water, stirring until mixture thickens. Do not boil. Cool. Stir in chocolate. Gradually beat in butter, 1 tablespoon at a time. Fold in nuts and vanilla, and stir until mixture is thick enough to spread. Yield: 1½ to 2 cups.

~

Bittersweet Chocolate Torte with Raspberries

14　1-ounce squares bittersweet or semi-sweet chocolate, coarsely chopped
½　cup butter
¼　cup whole milk
5　eggs
1　teaspoon vanilla
½　cup sugar
¼　cup all-purpose flour
¼　cup seedless red raspberry jam
2　cups fresh red raspberries
　　confectioners' sugar (optional)

Assemble ingredients and utensils. Grease bottom of 8-inch springform pan and set aside. In a heavy saucepan, combine chocolate, butter, and milk; cook and stir over low heat until chocolate melts. Remove from heat and cool about 15 minutes. In the large bowl of a mixer, beat eggs and vanilla on low speed until well combined; add sugar and flour, beat on high speed for 10 minutes. Stir chocolate mixture into egg mixture; pour into the prepared pan. Bake in a preheated 325° oven for 35 minutes or until torte is lightly puffed on the outer third of the top (because the torte is dense, the center will appear underbaked, but it's not). Cool in pan on wire rack for 20 minutes. While cooling, the torte may fall about ¼-inch in the center and may develop a brownie-like crusty surface. With a knife carefully loosen the torte from the sides of the pan. Cool completely about 2 to 3 hours. Remove the sides of the pan; wrap the torte in foil and chill overnight. To serve, bring the torte to room temperature. In a saucepan, melt the raspberry jam and spread jam on top of the torte. Top each serving with fresh raspberries and dust with confectioners' sugar. Yield: 14 to 16 servings.

A NOTE FROM

Miss Daisy

A torte is a rich cake, often made with little or no flour, but instead with ground nuts or breadcrumbs, eggs, sugar, and flavorings. Tortes are often multi-layered and filled with jam or butter cream.

Chocolate Valentine Torte

1½ cups sour cream
1¾ cups unsifted all-purpose flour
1¾ cups sugar
 ¾ cup unsweetened cocoa
1½ teaspoons baking soda
 1 teaspoon salt
 ⅔ cup butter or margarine, softened
 2 eggs
 1 teaspoon vanilla
    sliced almonds for garnish

Assemble ingredients and utensils. Heat sour cream in saucepan or microwave to lukewarm; set aside. In the large bowl of a mixer, combine flour, sugar, cocoa, baking soda, and salt. Blend in butter, heated sour cream, eggs, and vanilla on low speed. Beat 3 minutes on medium speed. Grease and flour two heart-shaped pans or two 9-inch round layer cake pans. Pour batter into pans. Bake in a preheated 350° oven for 30 to 35 minutes or until skewer inserted in center comes out clean. Cool 10 minutes; invert onto wire racks. Cool completely. Prepare vanilla cream filling or variations. With sharp serrated knife, cut layers in half horizontally. Place cut-side down; spread with one third of the filling. Top with cut layer, repeat procedure ending with plain layer on top. Prepare chocolate glaze; pour onto top of torte. Spread evenly allowing some to run down sides. Prepare decorator's frosting. Pipe onto top of cake. Garnish with sliced almonds, if desired. Yield: 8 to 10 servings.

Try these filling variations:

Strawberry: Decrease vanilla to 1 teaspoon; add ¾ teaspoon strawberry extract and 1 or 2 drops red food coloring.

Almond: Decrease vanilla to 1 teaspoon; add 1 teaspoon almond extract.

Cherry: Stir in ¼ cup chopped maraschino cherries, well-drained. Add 1 or 2 drops red food coloring.

A TIP FROM
Miss Daisy

Vanilla Cream Filling

¼ cup all-purpose flour, unsifted
½ cup whole milk
¼ cup butter or margarine, softened
¼ cup shortening
2 teaspoons vanilla
¼ teaspoon salt
4 cups confectioners' sugar

Assemble ingredients and utensils. Combine flour and milk in a small saucepan. Cook, stirring constantly with wire whisk, until mixture thickens and just begins to boil (mixture will be very thick); cool to room temperature. Cream butter and shortening until light and fluffy; add vanilla, salt and flour mixture. Gradually add confectioners' sugar, beating until spreading consistency. Yield: About 3 cups filling.

Chocolate Glaze

1 tablespoon butter
2 tablespoons unsweetened cocoa
2 tablespoons water
1 cup confectioners' sugar
¼ teaspoon vanilla

Assemble ingredients and utensils. Melt butter in small saucepan over low heat; add cocoa and water, stirring constantly until mixture thickens. Remove from heat; beat in confectioners' sugar and vanilla until smooth and of spreading consistency. Add additional water, ½ teaspoon at a time, if needed.

Decorator's Frosting

2 tablespoons butter, melted
2 tablespoons unsweetened cocoa
1 cup confectioners' sugar
½ teaspoon vanilla
1 tablespoon whole milk

Assemble ingredients and utensils. Combine all ingredients until smooth. Cool before piping onto the torte.

A TIP FROM

Miss Daisy

Say "love" deliciously with this Chocolate Valentine Torte.

Frozen Lemon Torte

3	cups Lemon Tea Cookies, crushed (see p. 24)
1	tablespoon butter
1	cup plus 4 tablespoons sugar
6	eggs, separated
8	tablespoons fresh lemon juice
¼	teaspoon lemon extract
	zest of 4 lemons, grated
2	cups heavy cream, whipped
	raspberries for garnish

Assemble ingredients and utensils. Reserve ½ cup of crushed lemon cookies and spread the remainder evenly over the bottom of a buttered 8x12-inch oven-proof glass dish or regular baking pan. Set aside. In a bowl, beat 1 cup sugar and egg yolks together, add lemon extract and zest. Pour this mixture into the top of a double boiler over hot (but not boiling) water, stirring constantly until mixture is thick. Cool, remove to a larger bowl, and fold in whipped heavy cream. In a small bowl, beat egg whites until stiff, add 4 tablespoons sugar, and fold into the lemon mixture. Pour mixture evenly over the crust and sprinkle with the remaining lemon cookies. Freeze for 6 hours or overnight; remove from freezer and let sit for 5 minutes. Cut into squares; top with dollop of whipped cream and a fresh raspberry before serving. Yield: 12 servings.

Orange-Pineapple Torte

1   18¼-ounce package yellow lite cake mix
2   1-ounce packages instant sugar-free vanilla
      pudding mix
4   egg whites
1   cup water
¼   cup vegetable oil
¼   teaspoon baking soda
1   cup skim milk, cold
1   8-ounce carton frozen lite whipped topping,
      thawed
1   20-ounce can unsweetened crushed pineapple,
      well drained
1   11-ounce can mandarin oranges, drained
      fresh mint for garnish

**HELPFUL
HINT**

**This light
dessert is
wonderful for
summer. It
looks lovely
served on a
beautiful
glass or
hand-painted
cake stand,
like the one
made by Gail
Pittman of
Jackson,
Mississippi,
that is
featured on
the cover.**

Assemble ingredients and utensils. In the large bowl of a
mixer, combine cake mix, 1 package pudding mix, egg whites,
water, oil, and baking soda; beat on low speed for 1 minute;
then beat on medium speed for 4 minutes. Pour into 2 greased
and floured 9-inch round cake pans. Bake in a preheated 350°
oven for 25 to 30 minutes or until a toothpick inserted near
the center comes out clean. Cool for 10 minutes; remove from
pans to a wire rack to cool completely. For filling, combine
milk and remaining pudding mix in a bowl and whisk for 2
minutes; let it stand for 2 minutes; fold in the whipped
topping. In a medium bowl combine 1½ cups pudding
mixture with pineapple and half of the oranges. Slice each
cake layer in half horizontally. Spread pineapple mixture
between the layers; frost the top and sides of the cake with
remaining pudding mixture. Garnish with remaining oranges
and mint. Yield: 12 servings.

Cherry Torte

Shell
3   eggs whites, room temperature
⅛   teaspoon salt
1   cup sugar
1   teaspoon vanilla
¾   cup walnuts, chopped
½   cup saltine cracker crumbs
1   teaspoon baking powder

Filling
1   16-ounce can pitted red cherries
¼   cup sugar
⅛   teaspoon salt
4   teaspoons cornstarch
1   cup heavy cream, whipped

Assemble ingredients and utensils. To make the shell, beat egg whites and salt together in small bowl of mixer until foamy. Gradually add sugar, 1 tablespoon at a time, and beat until stiff peaks form and the mixture looks glossy. Add vanilla. In a separate bowl, combine nuts, cracker crumbs, and baking powder. Fold this mixture into egg whites. Spread mixture in a well-buttered 9-inch pie pan, making a well in the center and building up the sides. Bake in a preheated 300° oven for 40 minutes. Remove from oven and cool. For filling, drain the cherries, reserving the juice. In a heavy saucepan, combine juice, sugar, salt, and cornstarch, mixing well; cook, stirring constantly, until mixture boils and is clear and thickened. Cool, then add drained cherries. To assemble, spread half of the whipped heavy cream over the torte; spread cherry mixture over the top, then garnish with remaining whipped cream. Chill for several hours before serving. Yield: 6 to 8 servings.

Blueberry Torte

2	cups graham crackers, crushed
1½	cups sugar
⅔	cup butter, melted
3	8-ounce packages cream cheese, softened
4	eggs
2½	teaspoons lemon zest, grated
1	pint blueberries
¼	cup water
1	teaspoon cornstarch, mixed with 2 tablespoons water

Assemble ingredients and utensils. Mix graham cracker crumbs, ½ cup sugar, and melted butter together in a bowl. Grease 8-inch springform pan. Press crumb mixture over the bottom and part-way up the sides of the pan. In a medium bowl, beat the cream cheese; add remaining sugar, eggs, and 2 teaspoons lemon zest; mix well. Pour mixture into crumb-lined springform pan. Bake in a preheated 350° oven for 30 to 35 minutes. Cool; it's best if chilled overnight. After torte is completely cooled, combine berries, water, cornstarch, and remaining lemon zest in a saucepan; simmer for a few minutes. Cool and spread over the torte. Yield: 12 servings.

Coconut Frosting and Filling

1   6-ounce can evaporated milk
⅔   cup sugar
¼   cup butter
1   egg, lightly beaten
⅛   teaspoon salt
1   teaspoon vanilla
1   3½-ounce can sweetened flaked coconut
½   cup pecans, chopped

Assemble ingredients and utensils. In a heavy saucepan, combine milk, sugar, butter, egg, and salt; cook and stir over medium heat until mixture thickens and begins to boil, 12 to 15 minutes, stirring constantly. Remove from heat; add vanilla, coconut, and pecans. Cool thoroughly. Yield: frosting for 2 9-inch layers or 1 10-inch bundt cake.

Vanilla Cream Filling

½   cup sugar
⅓   cup all-purpose flour
½   teaspoon salt
2   cups whole milk
2   eggs, lightly beaten
2   teaspoons vanilla

Assemble ingredients and utensils. In a heavy saucepan, mix sugar, flour, and salt; slowly stir in milk. Cook and stir over medium heat until mixture boils and thickens; cook 2 minutes longer. Stir a small amount of hot mixture into bowl with lightly beaten eggs. Add the egg mixture to remaining hot mixture, stirring constantly, bring just to boiling. Add vanilla. Cool. Yield: 2⅓ cups.

Variations
Chocolate Cream Filling: add 1½ 1-ounce squares unsweetened chocolate (cut up) with the milk and increase sugar to ¾ cup.
Butterscotch Cream Filling: use ⅔ cup brown sugar instead of granulated sugar and add ¼ cup butter with vanilla.

Old-Fashioned Seven-Minute Frosting

2	egg whites, unbeaten
1 1/2	cups sugar
2	teaspoons light corn syrup
1/3	cup cold water
1/8	teaspoon salt
2	teaspoons vanilla

Assemble ingredients and utensils. In the top of a double boiler, place all ingredients except vanilla. Beat 1 minute with electric or rotary mixer. Place over boiling water and cook, beating constantly, until frosting forms stiff peaks, about 7 minutes. Remove from heat. Pour into mixing bowl and add vanilla. Beat until spreading consistency, about 2 minutes. Yield: frosting for top and sides of 2 9-inch layers or 1 bundt cake.

Variation
Chocolate Fluff Frosting: Add 2 1-ounce squares unsweetened chocolate, melted and cooled, to Seven-Minute Frosting just before spreading on cake; fold it in, but do not beat.

Orange Frosting

1/2	cup sugar
2	teaspoons light corn syrup
1/8	teaspoon cream of tartar
1/4	cup water
1	egg white, stiffly beaten
1/4	cup confectioners' sugar
1	tablespoon fresh orange juice
1/2	teaspoon orange zest, grated

HELPFUL HINT

Orange Frosting is delicious on Devil's Food Cake! (see p. 106)

Assemble ingredients and utensils. In a heavy saucepan, combine sugar, corn syrup, cream of tartar, and water; heat and stir until sugar is dissolved. Cook syrup to 238°F on a candy thermometer. In a small bowl, gradually pour the syrup into beaten egg white, continuing to beat as you pour. Continue to beat for 10 minutes by hand until mixture thickens to spreading consistency. Stir in confectioners' sugar, orange juice, and zest. Yield: 1 1/2 to 1 3/4 cups frosting.

Chocolate Satin Frosting

3½ 1-ounce squares unsweetened chocolate
3 cups confectioners' sugar
4½ tablespoons hot water
1 egg
½ cup butter, softened
2 teaspoons vanilla

Assemble ingredients and utensils. In a heavy saucepan, melt chocolate. Place in mixing bowl and add sugar and water; mix continuously. Beat in egg; then butter and vanilla. The frosting will be thin at this point, so place your bowl in ice water and beat until it reaches spreading consistency. Yield: Frosting for bundt cake, or top and sides of 2 9-inch cake layers.

Caramel Icing

1½ cups brown sugar
¼ cup whole milk
2 tablespoons butter
1 teaspoon vanilla

Assemble ingredients and utensils. In a large saucepan, combine sugar, milk, and butter; bring to a boil and boil for 3 minutes, stirring constantly. Remove from heat; add vanilla. Cool to lukewarm. Beat until creamy and thick enough to spread. You can add a little cream if necessary to make it easier to spread. Yield: 1½ to 2 cups.

Lemon Sauce

3½ cups boiling water
2 tablespoons cornstarch
1½ cups sugar
¼ teaspoon salt
½ cup butter
¼ cup lemon juice
zest of 1 lemon, grated

HELPFUL HINT

This Lemon Sauce is a wonderful topping for Gingerbread (see p. 94).

Assemble ingredients and utensils. In a saucepan with 3½ cups boiling water, add cornstarch, sugar, and salt. Cook until thick and clear; continue cooking for 15 more minutes. Beat in butter, lemon juice, and lemon zest. Serve hot or cold. Yield: 2 cups.

Candies & Confections

SEVEN

Fantastic Fudge

HELPFUL HINT

Pack Fantastic Fudge in a gift tin for the holidays.

⅔ cup evaporated milk
⅔ cup butter or margarine
3 cups sugar
1 12-ounce package semi-sweet chocolate chips
1 7-ounce jar marshmallow creme
1 cup nuts, coarsely chopped
1 teaspoon vanilla

Assemble ingredients and utensils. Combine evaporated milk, butter, and sugar in a heavy 2½- to 3-quart saucepan. Bring to full rolling boil, stirring constantly to prevent scorching. Boil 5 minutes over medium heat or until candy thermometer reaches 234°F, stirring constantly. Remove from heat; stir in chocolate chips until melted. Add marshmallow cream, nuts, and vanilla; beat until well blended. Pour into greased 8- or 9-inch square pan. Cool; cut into squares. Yield: About 3 pounds fudge.

~

Chocolate Fudge Candy and Icing

2 cups sugar
¼ cup butter
½ cup margarine
⅔ cup whole milk
2½ squares semi-sweet chocolate
½ teaspoon vanilla

Assemble ingredients and utensils. Bring all ingredients to a boil, reduce heat to medium. Cook 3 minutes for icing, 5 minutes for fudge. Beat until thick. Spread icing on cake while hot, or pour into pans and cool for fudge. Yield: 2 pounds of fudge or enough icing for 1 cake.

Dark Chocolate Fudge

1 ¼   cups whole milk or half-and-half
4   1-ounce squares unsweetened chocolate, broken
     into small pieces
3   cups sugar
¼   cup light corn syrup
½   teaspoon salt
¼   cup butter
1   tablespoon vanilla

Assemble ingredients and utensils. In a heavy 3-quart
saucepan, cook milk and chocolate, stirring constantly until
chocolate melts and mixture is smooth. Blend in sugar, syrup,
and salt, stirring until sugar dissolves. Cook until candy thermometer registers 236°F (syrup forms soft ball in cold water).
Remove from heat and add butter and vanilla. Set saucepan in
cold water and cool to 110° without stirring. Beat vigorously
until candy holds its shape and begins to lose its gloss. Pour at
once into a buttered 9x9x2-inch pan; spread quickly into even
layer. Cool and cut into squares. Yield: 40 pieces.

Variations:
Chocolate Nut Fudge: Stir 1 cup pecan halves or coarsely
chopped walnuts into fudge with vanilla.
Marshmallow Fudge: Stir 1 cup miniature marshmallows into
fudge with vanilla.
Holiday Fudge: Stir ⅓ cup each red candied cherry halves and
chopped candied pineapple and ½ cup pecan halves into
fudge with vanilla.

A TIP FROM

Miss Daisy

Candy Temperature Chart
(using a candy thermometer)

Thread stage: 230°F to 234°F; spins a thread
when dropped from a spoon.

Soft ball stage: 234°F to 240 °F; forms a soft
ball when dropped in cold water.

Firm ball stage: 244°F to 248 °F; forms a firm
ball when dropped in cold water.

Hard ball stage: 250°F to 265°F ; forms a ball
hard enough to hold its shape when dropped in
cold water.

Cream Cheese Fudge

3   ounces cream cheese, softened
1   16-ounce box confectioners' sugar, sifted
3   tablespoons water
1   teaspoon vanilla
3   1-ounce squares unsweetened chocolate, melted
1   cup walnuts, chopped
    walnuts, whole for garnish

Assemble ingredients and utensils. In the large bowl of a mixer, combine cream cheese, sugar, water, and vanilla; blend until smooth. Quickly stir in melted chocolate and nuts. Turn into buttered 8x8x2-inch pan, spreading fudge about 1 inch thick. Chill. Cut in squares and top with additional walnuts. Yield: 15-24 pieces, according to cutting size.

~

Chocolate-Marshmallow Turtles

1½ cups semi-sweet chocolate chips
1   tablespoon vegetable shortening
12 large marshmallows
1½ cups pecan halves

Assemble ingredients and utensils. Melt chocolate chips and shortening in the top of a double boiler over hot (not boiling) water; remove from heat. Cool mixture to 85°F stirring constantly. Meanwhile, cut marshmallows in half horizontally; flatten with rolling pin. Set aside. On wax paper-covered tray, form head and hind feet of turtle by arranging 3 pecan halves with ends touching in center; for front feet, place 1 pecan quarter on each side of head. Arrange 24 of these clusters as bases for turtles. Spoon ½ teaspoon melted chocolate mixture into center of each cluster of pecans. To make turtle shell, place flattened marshmallow half in center of pecans on top of chocolate; press lightly to adhere. Spoon a small amount of chocolate onto marshmallow and spread with spatula to cover top and edges of marshmallow. Chill. Store covered in refrigerator. Yield: About 24 turtles.

Chocolate Truffles

½ cup heavy cream
⅓ cup sugar
6 tablespoons butter
1 cup semi-sweet mini chocolate chips
1 teaspoon vanilla
1 12-ounce package semi-sweet chocolate chips
2 tablespoons vegetable shortening

Assemble ingredients and utensils. Combine heavy cream, sugar, and butter in saucepan; bring just to a boil. Remove from heat; immediately add 1 cup mini chips. Stir until chips are melted; add vanilla. Pour into bowl; cool, stirring occasionally. Cover; chill in refrigerator several hours, preferably overnight, to allow mixture to ripen and harden. Form mixture into ½-inch balls working quickly to prevent melting. Place on wax paper-covered tray; cover loosely. Chill several hours. Prepare chocolate coating by melting remaining chocolate chips with shortening in the top of a double boiler over hot water (avoid getting water in chocolate). Cool to 85°F, stirring constantly. With fork, dip each truffle into chocolate; gently tap fork on side of bowl to remove excess coating. Invert truffle on wax paper-covered tray. Decorate top of coated center with small amount of chocolate. Repeat until all are coated. Chill completely. Yield: About 30 truffles.

HELPFUL HINT

When melting chocolate in a double boiler or custard cup, set it in a pan of water. Do not boil the water, as this will thicken or curdle the chocolate.

A TIP FROM
Miss Daisy

When making dipped candy, dip only one piece of chocolate at a time. Make sure the room temperature is cool. Keep chocolates out of steam. When the chocolate sets, store it in boxes lined with waxed paper. If chocolate thickens before you are finished dipping, put more water in bottom of a double boiler. After chocolates are ready, if chocolate becomes scratched in tin dish, you can redo chocolate by running a little warm water over it.

Chocolate Peanut Brittle

¼ cup unsweetened cocoa
1 teaspoon baking soda
1 tablespoon butter
1 cup sugar
½ cup light corn syrup
¼ cup heavy cream
1 ¼ cups salted peanuts

Assemble ingredients and utensils. Lightly butter a cookie sheet; set aside. Combine cocoa and baking soda in small bowl; add butter. Set aside. In a heavy 2-quart saucepan, combine sugar, corn syrup, and heavy cream. Place over medium heat and stir constantly until sugar is dissolved. Stir in peanuts. Continue cooking and stirring frequently until mixture reaches 300°F on candy thermometer (hard-crack stage). Remove from heat; stir in cocoa mixture. Immediately pour onto cookie sheet; quickly spread and pull into ¼-inch thickness. Place on wire rack to cool completely. Snap into pieces; store in airtight container. Yield: About 1 pound candy.

Peanut Butter Balls

HELPFUL
HINT

Peanut
Butter Balls
are a great
lunchbox
treat for
children and
adults alike!

~

1 cup peanut butter
⅓ cup instant nonfat dry milk
¼ cup sesame seeds
¼ cup raisins
¼ cup honey
½ cup unsweetened coconut

Assemble ingredients and utensils. In a large bowl, combine all ingredients. Form into balls. Chill and serve. Yield: 48 balls.

Peanut Butter Coconut Balls

1	12-ounce jar creamy peanut butter
1	cup flaked coconut
½	cup graham crackers, crushed
1½	cups pecans, chopped
1	16-ounce box confectioners' sugar
1	cup butter, softened
¼–⅓	block paraffin
1	6-ounce package chocolate chips

Assemble ingredients and utensils. In a mixing bowl, combine peanut butter, coconut, crumbs, nuts, sugar, and butter; mix well. Form into 1-inch balls. In the top of a double boiler or heavy saucepan, melt paraffin and chocolate chips. Using a toothpick, dip balls in chocolate mixture and cool on waxed paper. Yield: 72 pieces.

Peanutty Chocolate Pinwheels

1	12-ounce package semi-sweet chocolate chips
¾	cup sweetened condensed milk
¾	cup creamy peanut butter
1	tablespoon butter or margarine, melted
1	cup confectioners' sugar
3	tablespoons whole milk
1	teaspoon vanilla

Assemble ingredients and utensils. In a heavy saucepan, combine chocolate chips and sweetened condensed milk. Cook over low heat, stirring constantly, until melted and smooth. Remove from heat; cool slightly. Pat or spread evenly into 12x9-inch rectangle on wax paper; set aside. In the small bowl of a mixer, combine peanut butter and butter. Add confectioners' sugar, milk, and vanilla, beating until well combined. Pat or roll into a 12x9-inch rectangle on sheet of wax paper. Invert peanut butter onto chocolate; remove top sheet of wax paper. From long end, roll up jelly-roll style. Wrap tightly; chill until firm. Slice into ¼-inch slices. Yield: About 40 slices.

Minted Chocolate Drops

1   12-ounce package semi-sweet chocolate chips
2   tablespoons shortening
1   cup nuts, finely chopped
3   ounces cream cheese, softened
2   tablespoons butter
2   cups confectioners' sugar
1½   teaspoons vanilla
¼   teaspoon peppermint extract
5–6 drops red food coloring
5–6 drops green food coloring

HELPFUL
HINT

Pipe any
remaining
mint cream
onto wax
paper. You
can use it
later as a
garnish on
pies, cakes,
and mousses.

Assemble ingredients and utensils. In the top of a double boiler, melt chocolate with shortening until mixture is smooth. Stir in chopped nuts. Drop by slightly rounded teaspoonfuls onto wax paper-lined cookie sheet. Flatten slightly with spatula forming 1½-inch round drops about ¼-inch thick. Chill 5 to 10 minutes or until set. In a small bowl, combine cream cheese and butter until blended. Gradually add sugar, vanilla, and peppermint extract; beat until creamy. Divide mixture in half. Add red food color to one half; green to the other. Using a star tip pastry tube, pipe a rosette, or swirl a small amount of mint cream with a spatula onto top of each chocolate round. Chill to set. Yield: About 36 candies.

Party Mints

1   drop oil of peppermint
1   drop oil of wintergreen
½   cup butter
1   16-ounce box confectioners' sugar
1   tablespoon heavy cream
6–7 drops of food coloring (your choice)

Assemble ingredients and utensils. In a mixing bowl, combine all ingredients. Roll out in narrow strips. Leave in refrigerator for 1 hour. Cut into small pieces with candy cutter of choice. Yield: About 60, depending on size of candy cutter.

Pecan Dreams

1 cup butter, softened
½ cup confectioners' sugar
2¼ cups all-purpose flour
2 teaspoons vanilla
1 teaspoon water
1 cup pecans, chopped
  confectioners' sugar

Assemble ingredients and utensils. In the large bowl of a mixer, combine butter and sugar. Add flour, vanilla, and water; mix well. Add pecans. Place small balls of mixture on cookie sheet. Bake in a preheated 325° oven for 30 minutes. Roll in confectioners' sugar. Yield: 36 to 48 pieces.

~

Pralines

3 cups sugar
1 cup half-and-half
¼ teaspoon salt
2 tablespoons butter
1 tablespoon vanilla
2 cups pecan halves

Assemble ingredients and utensils. In a heavy saucepan over low heat, combine 2 cups sugar, half-and-half, salt, and butter, stirring often. In a small heavy saucepan, melt remaining 1 cup sugar over low heat. Pour the melted 1 cup sugar into hot sugar cream mixture very slowly, stirring constantly. Cook until a candy thermometer registers 236° F (syrup forms a small ball in cold water); remove from heat and stir in vanilla and nuts. Beat or stir until mixture begins to thicken. Drop rounded teaspoonfuls onto aluminum foil or waxed paper. Allow to cool and set; remove the foil or paper. Yield: 36 pieces.

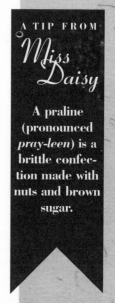

A TIP FROM

Miss Daisy

A praline (pronounced *pray-leen*) is a brittle confection made with nuts and brown sugar.

Snowballs

1 6-ounce package semi-sweet chocolate pieces
⅓ cup evaporated milk
1 cup confectioners' sugar, sifted
½ cup pecans, chopped
1 3½-ounce can flaked coconut

Assemble ingredients and utensils. In the top of a double boiler, combine chocolate and milk; heat over hot water until chocolate melts, stirring to blend. Remove from heat; stir in confectioners' sugar and pecans. Cool slightly. Form into 1-inch balls and roll in coconut. Yield: 24 snowballs.

Bourbon Balls

2 cups crushed vanilla wafers
1½ cups confectioners' sugar
4 tablespoons cocoa
1½ cups pecans, finely chopped
½ cup bourbon
¼ cup light corn syrup
   granulated or confectioners' sugar, or finely
      chopped pecans

Assemble ingredients and utensils. In a bowl, combine crushed vanilla wafers, sugar, and cocoa; stir in pecans. In a separate bowl, mix bourbon and syrup together; stir into crumb mixture and blend thoroughly. Shape rounded teaspoonfuls of mixture into balls. Roll balls in granulated or confectioners' sugar or in finely chopped nuts twice. Place on lightly greased (preferably butter) baking sheet; let stand uncovered in refrigerator for 2 hours to dry. Store in airtight container in cool place. Yield: 40 to 48 balls.

A TIP FROM

Miss Daisy

Snowballs are great on a buffet tray for holiday entertaining. They are beautiful garnished with a candied cherry on top and fresh greenery around them.

HELPFUL HINT

Bourbon Balls, a delicious confection that originated in Kentucky, will keep for several weeks if wrapped tightly in foil and refrigerated.

Appendices

A. Equivalents

Apples	1 medium	1 cup chopped
Bananas	1 medium	¾ cup sliced or ⅔ cup mashed
Breadcrumbs	2 slices	1 cup crumbs
Butter (or margarine)	1 pound	2 cups or 4 sticks
	½ pound	1 cup or 2 sticks
	¼ pound	½ cup or 1 stick or 8 tablespoons
Chocolate chips	12 ounce bag	1½ cups
Confectioner's sugar	1 pound box	4 cups
Figs, fresh	10 medium	1 cup chopped
Lemon	1 medium	2–3 tablespoons juice
Marshmallows	16 large	1 cup crème
Nut halves	4 ounces	Approximately 1 cup chopped
Orange	1 medium	⅓ cup juice
Pears	1 medium	⅔ cup sliced
Sweet potatoes	1 pound	1¼ cups mashed
Yeast	1 packet	2¼ teaspoons powder

B. Substitutions

1 1-ounce square chocolate	= ¼ teaspoon cocoa
1 tablespoon cornstarch	= 2 tablespoons all-purpose flour
1 cup all-purpose flour	= 1 cup less 2 tablespoons cake flour
1 cup whole milk	= ½ cup evaporated canned milk + ½ cup water
2 teaspoons active dry yeast	= 1 cake compressed yeast
1 cup sour milk	= 1 tablespoon vinegar plus milk to equal 1 cup

C. Measures & Weights

Dash or pinch	= less than 1/8 teaspoon
3 teaspoons	= 1 tablespoon
2 tablespoons	= 1/8 cup or 1 fluid ounce
4 tablespoons	= 1/4 cup
5 1/3 tablespoons	= 1/3 cup
8 tablespoons	= 1/2 cup
12 tablespoons	= 3/4 cup
16 tablespoons	= 1 cup or 8 fluid ounces
1 cup	= 8 ounces
2 cups	= 1 pint or 16 ounces
4 cups	= 2 pints or 1 quart or 32 ounces
2 pints	= 1 quart
4 quarts	= 1 gallon or 16 cups
16 ounces	= 1 pound
1 ounce	= 28.35 grams

D. Recommended Storage Periods

Baking powder and baking soda	8–12 months
Baking chocolate	6–12 months
Sweetened chocolate	2 years
Cornstarch	2–3 years
Dry yeast	18 months
Salad oil	6–9 months
Dried fruits	6–8 months
Nuts	1 year
Flour	9–12 months
Salt	indefinitely
Granulated and confectioners' sugar	indefinitely
Brown sugar	refrigerate and it will last longer

E. Terms

Beat: to whip by lifting a mixture up and over with a fork, spoon, wire whisk, rotary or electric beater.

Cream: to soften shortening or butter and blend with other ingredients by rubbing with a spoon or using an electric beater.

Cut in: to blend cold shortening with flour by cutting into flour with 2 knives or a pastry blender in a crisscross motion.

Caramelize: to stir granulated sugar over low heat until melted and brown in color.

Fold: to add ingredients, such as whipped cream or beaten egg whites, with a folding motion to preserve air bubbles. Remember when folding egg whites into a mixture, it is okay for some of the egg whites to show through.

Garnish: to add a decoration.

Grease: to coat with cooking spray, shortening, or butter.

Knead: to fold dough firmly with palms of hands, turning between folds.

Scald: to heat the liquid, usually milk, until hot but not boiling.

Stir: to blend ingredients with a circular motion.

Whip: to beat rapidly.

Index